THE AESTHETIC FACE OF BEING

THE AESTHETIC FACE OF BEING
Art in the Theology of Pavel Florensky

by
VICTOR BYCHKOV

Translated from the Russian
by
RICHARD PEVEAR AND LARISSA VOLOKHONSKY

Preface by
ROBERT SLESINSKI

ST VLADIMIR'S SEMINARY PRESS
Crestwood, NY
1993

Library of Congress Cataloging-in-Publication Data

Bychkov, V. V. (Viktor Vail'evich)
    [Esteticheskii lik bytiia. English]
    The aesthetic face of being: Art in the theology of Pavel Florensky / by Victor
Bychkov: translated from the Russian by Richard Pevear and Larissa
Volokhonsky.
      p.   cm.
    Includes bibliographical references.
    ISBN 0-88141-127-2
    1. Florenskii, P. A. (Pavel Aleksandrovich), 1882-1943—Aesthetics.
2. Aesthetics, Modern—20th century. 3. Aesthetics, Russian—20th century.
4. Aesthetics—Religious aspects—Orthodox Eastern Church—History of
doctrines—20th century. 5. Signs and symbols. 6. Icons—Cult. 7. Orthodox
Eastern Church—Doctrines.
I. Title.
BH221.R94F564413   1993
111'.85'092—dc20   93-15302
                                          CIP

THE AESTHETIC FACE OF BEING
Theology of Pavel Florensky

Translation copyright © 1993

by

ST VLADIMIR'S SEMINARY PRESS

ISBN 0–88141–127-2

PRINTED IN THE UNITED STATES OF AMERICA

Contents

Preface

The full importance of the life and work of Father Pavel Florensky (1882-1937) for Russian philosophical and theological thought is only beginning to be adequately apprised in our own time. For too long, especially in the West, he has been consigned to obscurity. His name, however, was never fully out of mind in his Russian homeland among those who cared for the type of integrated religious world view that he brought to the Russian Church during the critically important—and tragic—first three decades of this century. Indeed, interest in his life work and thought was shown in the public scholarly forum of the pre-*glasnost* Soviet Union, especially in the domain of semiotics, a camp seemingly less threatening to Marxist ears. Apart from the significance of this renewed interest in Florensky from the point of view of cultural history, this turn is important for a more complete understanding of Florensky's intellectual corpus in itself.

Up until relatively recently, knowledge of Florensky's work has largely been restricted to his metaphysical ideas and sophiological conception, which provide a philosophical world view for articulating his initial scholarly work in the fields of mathematics and empirical science. His fascination with the natural order motivated him to seek a deeper interpretation and over-arching synthesis of reality as immediately given to man in experience. On a personal level, this quest led Florensky to pursue seminary studies at the Moscow Theological Academy after several brilliant years as a student of mathematics at the University of Moscow, and eventually to accept Holy Orders in the Orthodox priesthood. On a theoretical level, two distinct advances can be found in Florensky's intellectual development. The first was devoted to his unique conception of the task of theodicy in which he passionately sought a root intelligibility to all the paradoxes of the order of the real. Until recently, virtually all of Florensky's published theological works, but especially his acclaimed work, *The Pillar and Foundation of Truth* (1914),[1] were devoted to this theme. This stage is rightfully called Florensky's sophiological period. At this point in his intellectual evolution, being for him is Sophia or cosmos.[2]

Already in his masterwork, however, Florensky points to the need to return from the heights of theodicy and sophiological speculation to anthropodicy which he viewed as nothing more than concrete metaphysics or a turn to man and world as *expressions* of the spiritual in the sensual or empirical order of being. Being here, for Florensky, is nothing other than "icon" or symbol. The author of the present work provides an excellent introduc-

1 The Moscow publishing house, *Pravda*, has just republished (1990) this work (*Stolp i utverzhdenie istiny*) as the first volume (in two installments) of a two-volume work. The second volume contains his later unfinished *U vodorazdelov mysli* (At the watersheds of thought).

2 For a detailed analysis of Florensky's position on this point, see our *Pavel Florensky: A Metaphysics of Love* (Crestwood, NY: St Vladimir's Seminary Press, 1984).

tion to this later stage of development in Florensky's thought. From sophiology, Florensky moved on to aesthetics and linguistics, finding at the core of both areas the reality of symbol: visual, on the one hand, verbal, on the other. Florensky's chief aesthetical ideas are argued in two capital works, *Iconostasis*[3] and *At the Watersheds of Thought.*[4]

In the meantime, the non-Russian reading public must content itself with secondary studies like the present one to enter into the richness of Florensky's seminal thought. Though lacking in full scientific apparatus due to technical reasons, the present popularization provides a wonderful indication of the renewed and vital interest among Russian scholars today in the Russian religious tradition, so long forgotten by the reigning ideology. This work is a faithful introduction to Florensky's aesthetics

3 First integrally published in *Bogoslovskie Trudy* (Theological Studies), IX (1972): 183-148. An abbreviated version of the same was published in the *Vestnik Zapadnoevropejskogo Patriarshego Ekzarkhata*, 65 (1960): 39-64. This latter version has been translated into English. See *Eastern Churches Review*, VIII (1976): 11-37.

4 See n. 1. It should be noted that YMCA Press, Paris, has published a volume also entitled *U vodorazdelov mysli*. This volume, the first volume of an intended collection of Florensky's works, is a collection of his articles on aesthetics, some of which were indeed planned for insertion in his own planned work with the same title. It also contains the integral text of *Ikonostasis* which was not intended by Florensky to be a part of this work. The YMCA Press volume also does not include any of the linguistic studies which form the core of *U vodorazdelov mysli*. For many decades, these studies lay unpublished in the Florensky family archives. Only the thaw of recent history has permitted these works to find suitable publication in their Russian original. Full English translations of these works, fortunately and at long last, are now in the offing.

and cannot but lead the reader to savor the beautiful as a primary datum, as one revelatory, i.e., symbolic, of the truth and goodness of being.

Robert Slesinski

Introduction

Aesthetics within the system of the Orthodox world view has followed a long historical path, which lies across several cultures, embraces many nations, and almost twenty centuries. Late antiquity, Byzantium, ancient Rus, the Russian religious revival of the late nineteenth and early twentieth centuries—these are the basic stages of the historical life of Orthodoxy and the development of its aesthetics. One can also point to the outstanding figures who contributed most to the formation of Orthodox aesthetic consciousness. There have been not a few of them in the course of two millennia, and they cannot all be regarded as Orthodox in the narrowly confessional sense of the word. Some of the creators of Orthodox aesthetics (in a broadly ecumenical sense) even lived outside the official sphere of Christianity, but objectively turned out to be among its authors.

Philo of Alexandria can undoubtedly be named as the forerunner and the first figure in the series. It ends and is crowned by the latest major father of the Orthodox Church, the great twentieth-century thinker, Pavel Florensky (1882-1937). The former was an older contemporary of Christ, who had not yet beheld the light of His teaching, but already anticipated Him and prepared theoretical paths for His countless disciples. The latter was conscious of himself as a God-chosen theoretician and practitioner of Orthodoxy, yet his powerful genius was too cramped by the traditional framework of an historically shaped confession. It is no accident that stern rigorists of the Orthodox Church even to this day doubt the orthodoxy of Fr. Pavel's spiritual legacy and regard many of his statements as all but heretical.

Between these two outstanding figures stands a long series of highly spiritual authors of Orthodox aesthetics, especially distinguished among them being Clement and Athanasius of Alexandria, the great Cappadocian fathers (Basil the Great, Gregory of Nyssa, Gregory the Theologian), John Chrysostom, the pseudo-Dionysius the Areopagite, John of Damascus, Theodore the Studite, the Fathers of the Seventh Ecumenical Council, the Patriarchs Germanus, Nicephorus, and Photius, Symeon the New Theologian, Gregory of Sinai, Gregory Palamas; in the Slavic world, John, the Exarch of Bulgaria; in Russia, the icon painter Andrey Rublev, Epiphanius the Wise, Nilus of Sora, Joseph of Volotsk, the fathers of the Council of a Hundred Chapters, the elders of Optina, Fyodor Dostoevsky, Vladimir Soloviev, and representatives of the spiritual revival of the beginning of the twentieth century, among whom the most important figure was undoubtedly Pavel Alexandrovich Florensky.

Taking a closer look at this bright constellation of names and this long period of development, it seems that western scholarship is right in reproaching Orthodoxy for its lack of a clearly formulated and consistently explained aesthetic system. Such a system is not to be found even in Pavel Florensky, though he was quite at home with the entire heritage of European-Mediterranean culture and philosophy, and virtually all of his numerous works on the most diverse subjects are pervaded with aesthetic intuitions, while his major theologico-philosophical work, *The Pillar and Foundation of the Truth*,* is, among other things, also a treatise on aesthetics. Here we encounter the most important and specific peculiarity of Orthodox aesthetics: it is essentially implicit, that is, not distinguished from, and not distinguishable from, the wholeness of culture as a living organism. Many Orthodox thinkers have been well aware of this, and Fr. Pavel felt it especially deeply.

Florensky is an outstanding and unique phenomenon in the history of Russian, and perhaps also world, culture. Indeed, he was the embodied quintessence of culture, its incarnate spirit, in a period of acute crisis. Much of what has been produced by Mediterranean culture over the past two or three thousand years was concentrated in his person in a certain harmonious wholeness. With equal ease and the most profound knowledge of the subject, Florensky occupied himself with physics and chemistry, mathematics and electronics, art history and museology, philology and philosophy, and many other disciplines, while always remaining a theologian and a priest—that is, a shepherd of souls, their guide on the paths of Truth, Good, and Beauty—for which the minions of Stalin's regime hated him and finally destroyed him.

"Fr. Pavel," wrote the well-known religious thinker of the beginning of the century, Sergei Bulgakov,**

* *The Pillar and Foundation of the Truth*, the third and final version of Pavel Florensky's dissertation for his Master's degree from Moscow Theological Academy, which he defended in 1912, was published by *Put'* (Moscow, 1914); volume IV of the YMCA Press edition of Florensky's works (Paris, 1989) is a reprint of this edition (referred to hereafter as *PFT*).

** Fr. Sergei Bulgakov's memoir, "The Priest Fr. Pavel Florensky," "was for me not only a manifestation of genius, but also a work of art—so harmonious and beautiful was his image. The word or brush or chisel of a great master is needed in order to tell the world about him... To speak of a genius who is indeed a sort of wonder of nature, one ought to be a genius oneself, or at least be capable of portraying his image with the power of penetration." These are the words of a contemporary and friend of Fr. Pavel, who through personal association had the chance to touch his spiritual world. But what are we to do, who, though compatriots and near contemporaries of the person of genius, are far from being geniuses ourselves and are separated from him by a bottomless gulf in our cultural tradition? How can we speak of this phenomenon, how can we today conceive and receive him—the quintessence of culture—in a world that has all but abandoned culture; him—the focus of spirituality—in a world that has forgotten the very notion of spirituality?

On the whole, it is perhaps impossible today to bring across to our contemporaries all the grandeur and significance of this man for the history of culture. It may be a matter for the future. The only thing left for us (but it is not so little!) is to study and comprehend Florensky bit by bit (Florensky the scientist, Florensky the art historian, Florensky the philosopher, and so forth), which is essentially what modern scholarship does with the whole of cultural history, treating literature, art, philosophy, religion, science separately, often forgetting that historically

written in 1943, was published in *Vestnik Russkogo Studencheskogo Khristianskogo Dvizhenia* (referred to hereafter as Vestnik), no. 101-102 (Paris, 1971), pp. 126-135. It is included as a preface in voume I of the YMCA Press edition of Florensky's works (Paris, 1985).

they constitute a living body whose life is defined precisely by its organic wholeness, by its essential unity and indivisibility. Of course, even this sort of analysis is not useless for the history of culture (the more so since modern scholarship is practically incapable of any other kind), but nevertheless it yields a fragmentary knowledge, and the sum of these fragments is still not a knowledge of the whole. This should be borne in mind by the reader of the present book as well. Though at this level aesthetics is perhaps the most advantageous discipline. It is, as we know, concerned with the higher forms of being, or, in Plotinus's words, with "the flower of being"; with the higher forms of relation between subject and object—the non-utile; with the highest state of the spirit—spiritual enjoyment. *Aesthetics is the science of the wholeness and perfection of being*—that is, perhaps the most universal of sciences. Therefore the analysis of the aesthetic consciousness, the aesthetic views and ideas of this or that stage in the history of a culture, a nation, a person, brings us closer than anything else to an understanding of the essence of any given cultural-historical phenomenon; gives us, if not a complete, at least a more or less coherent picture.

1

Beginnings

Every now and then nature sends into the world persons of a particular aesthetic gift, capable of feeling acutely (sometimes even painfully), of experiencing the lofty and the base, the beautiful and the ugly, the tragic and the comic—that is, the aesthetic in all its manifestations. In the history of Christian culture, the Blessed Augustine was such a person, and so, at the beginning of our century, was Pavel Florensky. From his memoirs, written with the pen of a great master, we learn that in early childhood he was particularly emotional and acutely receptive aesthetically. The main source and object of his aesthetic interest then was nature before all else; the first forms of his knowledge of the world were aesthetic forms.

The child Pavel, as far as he remembered himself later, was always in a state of heightened excitement from his ever-changing impressions. Florensky finds the most adequate expression of his childhood sense of himself in the image of a string played upon by nature's bow, from which an almost audible "high, pure, and taut sound" would vibrate through his whole body, and schematic images "like symbols of cosmic phenomena" would form

This chapter is based on Florensky, "Memoirs of Childhood, Religion, Nature," published in *Vestnik*, nos. 99-102 (Paris, 1970-1971).

themselves in his thoughts. Confessing to how "fiercely in love" with nature he was in his childhood, Fr. Pavel further explains that for him the whole natural kingdom was divided into two categories of phenomena—the "captivatingly gracious" and the "sharply particular." Both categories attracted and excited him, now with their refined beauty and spirituality, now with their mysterious unusualness. "The gracious, shot through with air and radiance, was light and intimately close. I loved it with all the fullness of tenderness, admiring to the point of cramped movement, of sharp pity, and asking why I could not merge with it entirely and, finally, why I could not take it forever into myself or myself enter into it." This piercingly sharp yearning of the child's consciousness, of his whole body, to merge entirely with a beautiful object, would be preserved ever after in Florensky, acquiring in maturity traditional Orthodox forms of the soul's yearning to merge with God.

In the child's consciousness, Nature lived its mysterious life hidden from people, and spoke with him as with its chosen favorite in the language of animal, vegetal, mineral forms, the forms of various natural phenomena. In various forms constantly revealed to him now here, now there, the impressionable boy caught the living gaze of Nature uncovering something hidden for him. Much later this gaze suddenly flashed for him from the eyes of his two-month-old son Vasya. "He opened his eyes and for a time looked consciously straight into my eyes, as neither he nor anyone else in my remembrance ever looked; to put it more correctly, this was a supra-conscious look, for it was not his small, unformed consciousness that looked at me through Vasya's eyes, but some higher consciousness, greater than I, or he, or all of us, that looked at me from the unknown depths of being. And then it all passed, and again before me were the eyes of a two-month-old infant."

The forms of manifestation of this "higher consciousness" in nature attracted and excited the future thinker from early childhood. "The whole world lived" by this consciousness, and the boy "understood its life" in its hidden foundation, understood not with reason, not with the mind, but with feeling, with deep aesthetic feeling. Analyzing his childhood experience, the learned man Florensky observed: "For indeed the perception of a child is of a more aesthetic character than the scientific, or at least pseudo-scientific, perception of an adult." The young Pavel's aesthetic perception was particularly acute.

Wayside blooms, buds, leaf-buds attracted him more than the luxuriance of fully opened flowers. The beauty of the bud fascinated him with its mystery, its promise, the possibility of another as yet unfolded life, of another, as yet unapparent, but ripening being.

In little Pavel's attitudes toward nature one can clearly sense that sacred trembling with which ancient man, with his primordial mythological consciousness, looked upon the natural world around him. To this consciousness which did not separate itself from the world or oppose itself to it, amazing secrets of creation were revealed, astonishing aspects of things and relations between them, deep-seated archetypes and essential foundations of being. Remnants of this consciousness are preserved in many children, but few remember them once they have grown up or pay any serious attention to them.

One needs a special gift of spiritual and aesthetic sensitivity to preserve these revelations of a pure, childlike, and at the same time, very ancient consciousness in one's soul and to be aware of them as something very important. That they occur regularly and are, in essence, objective, is attested to in memoirs of the childhood impressions of many artistically gifted people.

Hermann Hesse, for example, one of the most important writers of this century, and a man of acute aesthetic feeling, describes in his story "An Iris" a boy named Anselm, whose relationship with nature is remarkably close to that of the young Florensky. Anselm, too, is excited by many phenomena of nature, particularly the mystery of flowers, the elusive depths opening in them. Gazing at a beautiful iris, he "saw among the little golden posts a blue path with light veins leading into the heart, into the secret of secrets of the flower, where he knew the essence he was searching for was to be found..." Penetrating to the depth of the flower, his soul peeks through those gates where a phenomenon becomes a riddle, and vision—providence.

No less acute than his receptiveness to natural phenomena was the young Pavel's receptiveness to certain phenomena of art, the auditory above all—music, poetry. Music, Florensky confessed, so greatly shook his consciousness as a child that his frenzied love for it sometimes turned into hostility. In those days he considered the works of Mozart and Beethoven to be the standard of true musicality, approaching the music that constantly sounded in the ears of the impressionable, spiritually gifted boy. What he valued in music was not psychological, but something deeper, more ontological. Later in life he described his childhood impressions: "It sounded in my consciousness like the music of the spheres, like the formula of the world's life." When, as a mature man, Fr. Pavel became acquainted with the music of Bach (which was not so well-acknowledged in Russia at the turn of the century as it is now), he recognized in it something very close to what had sounded in him throughout this childhood years.

In singing, which the young Pavel especially loved, he was attracted not by the words—he usually did not understand them—and not by the melody, but by something hidden behind and beneath them. "For me, what was most attractive and worthy of attention was the manifestly irrational—that which I really did not understand, and which rose up before me like an enigmatic hieroglyph of a mysterious world." For example, the height of graciousness for him was the romance by Glinka to the words of Pushkin's "I Remember the Wondrous Moment," in which, as the epitome and essence of beauty, there soared up the mysterious and incomprehensible word "asagenis" (a child's perception of the phrase "as a genius"). Profoundly sensing in this word "a symbol of beauty's infinity," the child deliberately did not try to find out what it meant in ordinary language, afraid of destroying the charm of the mysterious combination of sounds.

Having grown wise with experience, the thinker Florensky would see in this childhood perception a correct approach to the essence of art, of the artistic in general: "And perhaps the artistic fulfillment of verse, music, and all the rest, indeed, lies in the fact that their supra-logical content, without destroying the logical, nevertheless immeasurably exceeds it, and, being a language of spirits, is accessible to a child's generally non-rationalizable perception to an even greater degree than to an adult's."

In verse the young Pavel was also attracted first of all by the musical aspect, which in his perception dominated the logical meaning. He would rapturously recite meaningless verses and monologues, seizing on sonorous combinations of unintelligible geographical or historical names and foreign words, mostly Italian, French, and Spanish. Usually, Florensky wrote, he preferred to do this alone in a semi-dark little room, while his mother and nanny were giving one of his sisters a bath: "...to start something like a conversation first, in a strange language with sonorous words, interspersed with meaningless, but sonorous, combinations of syllables; then, becoming inspired, to begin a melodramatic declamation of the same sort, and finally, in complete self-abandon, to pass over to glossolalia, confident that the very sound I uttered expressed in itself my contact with a far-off, graciously refined, exotic world." This childish "zeal," as Florensky put it, brought the boy to a state of ecstasy. It is close in character to the sacral-aesthetic meditation proper to many ancient pagan cults, with an obvious predominance of the aesthetic element.

From early childhood Florensky felt that the aesthetic (the gracious and refined, in his child's perception) is the expression and the bearer of something mysterious, vitally important, essential. And he kept this feeling throughout his life, constantly turning to the sphere of the artistic and the aesthetic in his studies of the most diverse aspects of culture. One can also understand in this sense his love of ancient Greece and of classical art. According to one witness, the walls of the priest Florensky's room in Sergiev Posad were covered with photographs of Greek statues. In the beauty of Greek plastic art he perceived considerably more than the mere external beauty of the body. The beauty of art, as we shall see further on, was for Fr. Pavel always a bearer, an expression, a symbol of the spiritual principle.

"Every phenomenon on earth," wrote Hermann Hesse, "is a symbol, and every symbol is an open gate through which the soul, if it is ready to do so, can penetrate to the depths of the world, where you and I, day and night, become one. Now and then on life's path every man finds the open gate, to each the thought comes at some point that everything visible is a symbol, and that behind the symbol dwell the spirit and eternal life. But few are those who enter the gate and resign the beautiful appearance for the sake of the perceived reality of the depths." Aesthetic phenomena are perhaps the widest and most available gates to the spiritual realm; they opened very early for the young Pavel, and he, without much thinking, with all the rapture and self-abandon of a child, rushed through them, sensing beyond them an endless series of other gates, leading to the hidden sources of being.

2

The Aesthetic

In his maturity, Pavel Florensky gave the closest attention to the sphere of the aesthetic. He strove to comprehend its numerous phenomena, to define their place in the system of culture, and he spent much time reflecting, writing, and lecturing on art.

The aesthetic, for Florensky, is not some localized part of being or consciousness, nor is it a specific property of being. For him, as for the main line of traditional Orthodoxy, it is a certain energy pervading the whole of being, almost identical with spirituality, and virtually eluding formalization—that is, verbal, not to mention systematic, expression. Accordingly, the aesthetics of Florensky, as of the whole of historical Orthodoxy, can be reconstructed with only approximate precision on the basis of a profound study of his spiritual legacy.

In opposing his understanding of "aestheticity" to the concept of the nineteenth century Russian writer Konstantin Leontiev, Florensky clearly formulates his aesthetic position: "Thus for Leontiev 'aestheticity' is the most general characteristic, while for the author of the present book it is the deepest. There, beauty is only the

This chapter is based on *PFT*, chapters 3, 10, 11 and 17; on *Nebesnie Znameniya* ("Heavenly Signs") and *Troitse-Sergiyeva Lavra I Rossiya* ("The Trinity-St Sergius Monastery and Russia"), both included in vol. I of the YMCA Press edition.

shell, the outermost of the various 'longitudinal' layers of being, while here it is not one of many 'longitudinal' layers, but a force that cuts through all layers. There, beauty is furthest of all from religion, but here it is expressed most of all in religion. There, the understanding of life is atheistic, or almost atheistic, whereas here God is precisely the Highest Beauty, through communion with Whom everything becomes beautiful...And while in Leontiev beauty is almost identified with Gehenna, with non-being, with death, in the present book beauty is Beauty and is understood as Life, as Creativity, as Reality."

This is perhaps Florensky's fullest and most important formulation of his understanding of the *aesthetic*, from which it becomes clear what great significance he ascribed to it and why aesthetics in Orthodoxy does not have the status of an independent discipline. Its subject is virtually indistinguishable from the subject of theology. "Everything is beautiful in a person when he turns toward God, and everything is ugly when he is turned away from God." It can be seen from this quotation that Fr. Pavel all but identifies the aesthetic with beauty and sees its highest limit, within the tradition of Christian aesthetics, in God.

Aesthetics in Florensky's work is inseparable from ontology and gnoseology, and the aesthetic phenomenon from knowing and from being itself. In turn, the act of knowing for him (as for all of Orthodoxy) is not only a gnoseological—that is, an ideal—act, but also ontological, an act of being. "Knowing," he wrote, following patristic tradition, "is a real act of going out of himself by the knower, or, which is the same, a real going out of that which is being known into the one who knows—a real unity of the knower and the known. This is a basic and characteristic postulate of all Russian philosophy and of Eastern philosophy generally." Knowing is understood by Florensky not as a unidirectional activity of the knowing subject, but as an equal and mutual striving of subject and object, a "living and moral communion of persons each of whom serves the other as both subject and object." He is speaking here, of course, not of some partial knowledge such as the scientific knowledge of particular aspects of being, or the philosophical knowledge of the laws of thinking and so on, but of a complete, full, and absolute knowledge—a knowledge of the Truth in its fullness and essential foundations. For Christianity this Truth is concentrated in the personal, tri-hypostatic God, and it is Him that Florensky has in mind as the limit of human knowledge.

Thus knowledge of the Truth is conceivable only as a real union with it, which is possible only "through the transubstantiation of man, through his deification, through the acquisition of love as the divine essence,"— that is, through a *real* change in the very essence of man, his transition to a different quality. And this sacral act of the highest knowing is possible only as an *act of love*; indeed, Florensky understands it as love itself. "In love and in love alone is a real knowledge of the Truth conceivable." Love—as Fr. Pavel constantly emphasizes—is understood here not psychologically, but purely ontologically. It is a real merging of the subject and the object of knowing, implying the essential transfiguration of the subject, his deification, together with the entrance of the known into the knower.

The integral sacral act of *knowing-love-transubstan-tiation* has three aspects—gnoseological, ethical, and aesthetic—which in fact form an ontological whole. "That which for the subject of knowing is truth, for its object is love, and for one who contemplates it [from outside—V.B.] this knowing is beauty." In Florensky's understanding, the metaphysical triad of *Truth, Good, and Beauty* is formed not of different principles or aspects of being, but of *one principle*. It is one and the same *spiritual life* considered from different angles. Spiritual life centered in the subject of knowing is Truth. Understood as the "direct action" of the object of knowing, it is the Good. "As an object of contemplation by a third person, as radiating outside—it is Beauty."

Thus the aesthetic aspect presupposes a certain third, external position, that of the observer, a position which in principle coincides neither with the subject nor with the object of being-knowing—a disinterested person, a non-utilitarian (if the utilitarian is understood as the very striving for knowledge) contemplator. In other words, the subject strives to possess the Truth and creates the situation of knowing; the Truth actively desires to be known and generates the atmosphere (or state) of love. "Realized love" appears to the outside observer as beauty.

In the universe, this love manifests itself as the love of the Creator for His creature and is objectively perceived as beauty. In other words, the beauty of the God-created world is the manifestation of divine love for the world. "Hence the pleasure, the joy, the comfort love brings when it is contemplated. That which brings joy is called beauty; love as the object of contemplation is beauty." Here an essential aspect of beauty is revealed—a subjective one, or an aspect of spiritual hedonism. Beauty as the realized love of God brings pleasure, "gladness" to him who contemplates it, and thereby reveals itself in the third element—the subject of aesthetic perception.

The actions corresponding to this at the social level—the relations of persons within Christian society—are also seen by Florensky in the light of divine love and the knowledge of God. The norm of these relations, as we know, is love, understood by Fr. Pavel as "the con-substantiality of those who love in God," when each "I" is identical to every other "I" and at the same time different, when two loving persons forming a unity in which neither side loses its personal principle. "This dyad has love for its essence, which being a concretely embodied love, is beautiful for objective contemplation"—that is, for a third "I" it appears as beauty. Thus there emerges as an element of Christian society a distinctive triad of lovers. The third "I," "contemplating the dyad objectively," becomes inflamed with love for a fourth "I" and forms the basis, the first "I," for a new triad, and so on. As a result, all these triads knit together "into a consubstantial whole—the Church, or the Body of Christ, as an objective revealing of the Hypostases of divine love."

Each member of the social triad has its own spiritual life within itself: for the first, knowledge; for the second, love; for the third, pleasure. Their ways toward God differ accordingly.

Thus the *aesthetic*, characterized by the notions of *beauty* and *pleasure* is, in Florensky's system, a most important component of social and cosmic being (along with truth and love, or the gnoseological and the ethical). Undoubtedly, for the twentieth century, Fr. Pavel was an inspired bearer of Orthodox consciousness, for which the tri-unity of these forms of spiritual life has always been axiomatic and yet has perhaps never received such clear-cut verbal expression as in his *Pillar and Foundation of Truth*.

With regard to knowing, the subject of knowing may be and often is also the subject of aesthetic perception. This concerns, first of all, the knowledge of the tri-hypostatic Truth in the act of divine revelation. When the grace of the Holy Spirit descends upon him who thirsts to know the Truth, it is in the Holy Spirit that he "contemplates the ineffable beauty of the divine essence" and "rejoices with inexplicable trembling, seeing in his heart the 'intelligent light' or the 'light of Tabor'; and he himself becomes spiritual and beautiful." The third hypostasis of the Holy Trinity (according to Florensky, who rests upon Church tradition) is the source and cause of the beauty that is revealed to the believer and transforms him according to His likeness. The basic form in which it expresses itself is 'intelligent light' or the 'light of Tabor'—that is, according to late Byzantine mystical tradition, the uncreated light of the divine essence, which Christ showed to His beloved disciples on Mount Tabor in the act of the "Transfiguration." This light is the light of Truth; in it "the form of truth and the content of truth are one." Here we find in Florensky the virtual unity of the aesthetic and the highest gnoseology, which is of great importance for understanding the two forms of spiritual activity. The main unifying factor is the light of Tabor, in which content and form are identical and which, being the bearer of Truth and *truth* itself, is perceived as *beauty*.

In affirming the unity of light and beauty, Florensky indeed completes many centuries of Neoplatonic-Christian tradition. To explain this most important tenet of Christian aesthetics to his contemporaries, who had largely lost the capacity for spiritual vision, he turns to physical light. In it he sees the main property of the beautiful—*self-worth*. All else in the material world is beautiful not in itself, not objectively, but through a certain "intellectual satisfaction" it gives to man, which is based on proportion of formal parts, rhythmical constitution, and so on. "Whereas light is beautiful beyond all fragmentation, beyond form; it is beautiful in itself, and through itself makes beautiful all that appears."

Beauty as a certain kind of "revealing of that which becomes objective," as a factor of objectivization, is essentially connected with light, for "all that is revealed is revealed through light." And Florensky understands this *revealability* not so much in a psychological sense (though, in principle, this is not denied) as in an *ontological* sense, confirming it by references to the apostle Paul. This basis also makes understandable his transition to absolute Beauty and spiritual light. "Thus, if beauty is precisely revealability, and revealability is light, then, I repeat, beauty is light and light is beauty. The absolute light is then the absolutely beautiful—Love itself in its completeness, which (through itself) makes every person spiritually beautiful. The Holy Spirit, who crowns the love of the Father and the Son, is both the subject and the organ for contemplating the beautiful."

This understanding of beauty in Fr. Pavel's writings makes of spiritual elders and ascetics its deepest connoisseurs, since they devote themselves solely and exclusively to contemplation of the "ineffable light." They are, in fact, the major aesthetic subjects, and asceticism emerges in a direct sense as Orthodox aesthetics. It is no accident, Florensky emphasizes, that "the holy fathers called asceticism not science, not even moral work, but art, and, moreover, art par excellence, the 'art of arts.'" The main fruit and goal of this art is a special, non-formalizable knowledge, "contemplative knowledge," which, to distinguish it from theoretical knowledge—φιλοσοφία ("love of wisdom")—is called φιλοκαλία ("love of beauty"). This is precisely why collections of ascetic writings were called "philokalia." Fr. Pavel finds the Russian translation of the term, *dobrotoliubie* ("love of goodness"), not very successful. It would be more precise to call these works "Love of Beauty," or else to take the word *dobrota* ("goodness") of the accepted translation not in its modern, but in the ancient, more general sense, "signifying beauty rather than moral perfection." And he adds in conclusion: "Undoubtedly the basic moment of the concept of *dobrotoliubie* ('love of goodness'), as well as of the Greek φιλοκαλία, is artistic, aesthetic, and not moral."

"Love of beauty" not only opens the ascetic to special knowledge, but unites him with beauty *in reality*. Asceticism, Florensky thinks, "creates" not so much a "good" man as a "beautiful" one. In this lies its specific quality. The distinctive feature of holy ascetics is not at all their "goodness," which even sinful people may possess, "but spiritual beauty, the dazzling beauty of the radiant, light-bearing person, which is by no means accessible to the dense and fleshly man." The science of the "love of beauty" enables a man to achieve *transfiguration* of the flesh, to acquire the original beauty of creation while still in this earthly life. The face of an ascetic really becomes the "life-bearing face," "all that is unexpressed, unminted;" it "becomes an artistic portrait of itself, an ideal portrait, fashioned out of living material by the loftiest of arts, the 'art of arts.'" This face strikes everyone by its radiance and beauty, which bear out the "inner light" of the ascetic. It is precisely in the *real creation of beauty* that Fr. Pavel perceives one of the most important meanings of aesthetics.

Hence, for Florensky, the holy ascetics—experts and connoisseurs of true beauty—are also the most important judges for evaluating the truth of spiritual life, its "churchness" (*tserkovnost'*). For he regards beauty as the criterion of "correctness" for this life—"that particular spiritual beauty which, while eluding logical formulas, is at the same time the only right way of defining what is Orthodox and what is not."

The aesthetics of asceticism, as we know, began to take shape among Christian desert dwellers and monks in the fourth century and continued to perfect itself during the whole history of Byzantium, Mount Athos, and later in ancient Rus, but it was formulated most clearly and precisely by Fr. Pavel Florensky at the beginning of our century. In the holy ascetics he finds the focal point, the concentration of the aesthetic that is spread throughout the world.

Referring to an important ascetic of the fourth century, Macarius of Egypt, Florensky stresses that a monk, an ascetic (*inok* in Russian), is different (*inoi*) from ordinary "worldly" people. He possesses a different mind, a different wisdom from the wisdom of this world, and the whole world appears differently to his consciousness.

"Leaving worldly life, the monk gives himself to the life of the world." For him, all the ordinary cares and hopes of men lose their significance; he simply does not notice them. The whole created world is revealed to him in a new light, in a new sense. The monk now sees in all things and phenomena "the signs and scripture of God," reading which he perceives the unfolding light of Truth.

By this light, as has already been pointed out, he himself is enlightened both spiritually and physically. Perceiving the light of the highest knowledge, the ascetic "lights up" and also transforms bodily. Through his face, subject to the imprint of time, the beautiful *countenance* of the first-created image, as he was intended by the Creator and which he should acquire upon the resurrection of the dead, begins to shine. The faces of many ascetics—and here Florensky quotes evidence from the wealth of hagiographic literature—were transfigured, and gave out a visible radiance while they were still alive. It was this actual radiance that became the basis for the firm tradition of portraying saints with a halo, nimbus, or glory around their heads.

However, in leaving the world, the monk does not become shut up solely and exclusively in himself. He abandons the world of vanity, petty squabbles, carnal lusts, and the false consumer life, so that, having transfigured himself spiritually and physically through the ascetic life, he may return as a bearer of the true values he perceives in this same world.

Asceticism does not reject the body, the flesh— Florensky emphasizes this more than once—rather it fights with carnal lusts for the transfiguration of the flesh and its final *deification*, its elevation to a divine state.

Hence the highly developed love of ascetics for the creaturely world, for every creature. Florensky never tires of copying out pages and pages from the sayings of ancient ascetics about their joy in contemplating the creaturely world, the tender tears of their love for this world, the purity of heart "that pities every creaturely being," the heart "aflame for the whole of creation"—sayings about people, animals, and birds, about reptiles and even demons; about their prayers for every creature, and first of all for every sinful man.

The entire creaturely world is revealed to the inner eye, to the hearts of the ascetic, as an eternal wonder of God, as "one living being praying to its Creator and Father." And there is nothing blameworthy in this being. Asceticism—Fr. Pavel underscores—does not deny the visible beauty of the world, of the creature, of the human body, but perceives in it traces of the first-created beauty, the wisdom of the Creator, which is inconceivable for our minds.

Florensky quotes a story from St John Climacus about an ascetic who was moved to tears at the sight of a beautiful woman's body and began to burn with still greater love for God who created this beauty. Thus, Fr. Pavel concludes, the goal of the ascetic life is the attainment of "incorruption and deification of the flesh through acquisition of the Spirit," one of the evidences of this acquisition being the gift of seeing beauty. Hence "the aim to which the ascetic aspires is to perceive every creature in its first-created, victorious beauty. The Holy Spirit reveals Himself in the ability to see the beauty of creation. To always see the beauty in everything would mean 'to resurrect before the general resurrection' [the

quotation is from St John Climacus—V.B.], would mean
to anticipate the final Revelation—the Comforter." Thus
the monastic endeavor should be crowned by the acquisition of the Holy Spirit, who enlightens and transforms
man spiritually and physically, makes him beautiful and
capable of perceiving beauty. "The spirit-bearing person
is beautiful," writes Florensky, "and twice beautiful. He
is beautiful objectively, as an object of contemplation for
those around him; he is also beautiful subjectively, as the
focus of a new, purified contemplation of what surrounds
him." The ascetic is thus simultaneously an object and a
subject of the aesthetic. By means of ascetic endeavor he
has transfigured himself, thereby disclosing to those who
contemplate him "his beautiful, first-created being." On
the other hand, in the process of his spiritual enlighten-
ment, the first-created beauty of the universe is disclosed
"to the saint's contemplation. He reveals beauty in himself, he abides in beauty, and he contemplates beauty."
Such, in Fr. Pavel's view, is the life of a true member of
the Church, for "*tserkovnost'* is the beauty of a new life
in absolute beauty—the Holy Spirit."

Thus the holy ascetic, entering into real communion
with the life of "absolute beauty," in fact overcomes in
this lifetime the boundary between the two worlds of the
universe: the one below and the one above. And he per-
forms this most complex ontological metamorphosis on
the level of the aesthetic, on the path of the love of
beauty—philokalia. The loftiness and significance of this
action are witnessed to by the fact that, according to
Florensky, the ascetic is in this way actually raised to the
level of Sophia, for it is she "who is the first-created
nature of the creature, the creative Love of God."

In Fr. Pavel's ontology, Sophia—the Divine Wisdom—is precisely that highest of creatures who overcomes the boundary between what is above and what is below, uniting these worlds through herself. She is "the Great Root of all creation...through which creation reaches into the inner life of the Trinity, and through which it receives Everlasting Life from the One Source of Life." Sophia, in Florensky's understanding, is a sort of indefinable state of transition from God to creature; she is no longer God, the divine light, but not yet a creature, "not the coarse inertia of matter"; she is a certain "metaphysical dust" hovering "on the ideal boundary between the divine energy and creaturely passivity; she is as much God as not God, and as much creature as not creature. One can say neither 'yes' nor 'no' about her..." Sophia is the first and subtlest product of God's activity. And for the creaturely world she is a focus of the creative energy that fertilizes art—that is, the aesthetic activity of man—and is therefore an important link in the aesthetic system of Orthodoxy.

Reflecting on Sophia, Florensky recalls that she appeared to the future enlightener of the Slavs, Constantine-Cyril, the philosopher, still in his adolescence, in the image of "a most beautiful maiden of royal appearance," and Cyril carefully bore this symbol with him throughout his life, giving it to the Slavs as well. "And this symbol became the first essence of the infant Russia that was to receive of the royal bounties of Byzantine culture." The second "symbol of the Russian spirit," formed this time on Russian soil, was in Florensky's view, as we know, the icon of the Trinity by Andrey Rublev.

Sophia, according to Florensky, participates in the

life of the tri-hypostatic Divinity, is in communion with
the divine love, and is closely connected with the second
hypostasis—the Word of God. Independently of Him
"she has no life and crumbles into fragmentary ideas
about creation; but in Him she acquires creative power."
For Orthodox consciousness, Sophia's being in the world
appears in a multitude of aspects. In man it shines through
as the image of God, his original beauty. In the God-man
Christ it is the beginning and the center of the redemption
of creation—His body, that is, the creaturely principle in
which the Divine Word was incarnated. Sophia is also
understood as the Church in its heavenly and earthly
aspects. In the latter case, she appears as the totality of all
those who have begun the endeavor of restoring their lost
divine likeness. And since the process of purification of
the Church's members is realized by the Holy Spirit,
"Sophia is the Spirit, because He deified creation." But
the Spirit of God reveals Himself in the creaturely world
as virginity, inner integrity, and humble chastity. Therefore Sophia is virginity. And her bearer in the final and
highest sense is the Virgin Mary, the Mother of God,
whom Florensky identifies with Sophia.

The many aspects of Sophia in the creaturely world
have a single deep root—*spiritual beauty*, the incorruptible, first-created *beauty of creation*. Sophia is "the true
adornment of the human being, which penetrates through
all his pores, shines in his eyes, flows out with his smile,
exults in his heart in ineffable joy, is reflected in his every
gesture, surrounds him in moments of spiritual uplifting
with a fragrant cloud and a radiant nimbus, makes him
'higher than the world's union,' so that while remaining
in the world he becomes 'not of the world,' becomes

supra-worldly...Sophia is Beauty." Sophia is the spiritual principle in the creaturely world and in man which makes them beautiful; it is the essential basis of the beautiful. "Sophia alone," wrote Florensky, "is the essential Beauty in all creation; the rest is mere trumpery."

The first and chief bearer of Sophia on earth, for Orthodox consciousness, is the Mother of God—the living intermediary between heaven and earth, the above and below. "As the Spirit is the Beauty of the Absolute, so the Birthgiver of God is the Beauty of the creaturely, 'the glory of the world,' and by her the whole of creation is adorned." The Orthodox world received the Mother of God as a symbol of the spiritual principle on earth, as a real manifestation of Sophia, as the comforter and Intercessor for sinful mankind before God, as the heavenly Jerusalem descended to earth, as "the center of creaturely life, the point of contact between heaven and earth," as one endowed with cosmic power. "In the Mother of God, the power of Sophia—that is, angelic power—is combined with human lowliness." She stands on the line separating Creator from creature and is therefore utterly inconceivable. The main evidence of her Sophianity is her ineffable beauty, which illumines the whole creaturely world and fills the hearts of men with indescribable joy. Man's yearning to grasp this beauty can be clearly seen in iconographic art: "Iconography gives many particular aspects of the Sophian beauty of the Virgin Mary."

Thus, for Florensky, the sphere of the aesthetic, the sphere of beauty in its subtlest forms of manifestation, but which are still accessible to perception, is first of all the sphere bordering between the world above and the world below. Sophia as the bearer of the Holy Spirit, most fully perceivable in the Mother of God, descends to it from the world above. And from the creaturely world it is profoundly and consistently inculcated by the ascetic monks who dedicate themselves to serving Beauty. However, asceticism, though important, is not the only way of overcoming the boundary between the two worlds from below; it is not the only way of ascent to Beauty. Florensky points to other ways, such as dreams, certain forms of art, and the cult of the Church.

3

Art

In considering the individual ascent of the soul to the invisible world, Florensky points to dreams that wander somewhere on the border which simultaneously joins and separates the two worlds. He distinguishes between two kinds of dreams, those of the evening and of the dawn. The first have a mainly psychological character, reflecting the impressions accumulated in the soul during the day; the second are mystical, "for the soul is filled with night consciousness," the experience of visiting the heavenly spheres. The first emerge as the soul ascends from the world below to the world above, and are images and symbols of the world it has just left; the second are symbols of heavenly visions.

This process accompanies any transition from sphere to sphere, creative art in particular, when the soul "is taken up from the world below and ascends to the world above. There, without images, it is nourished by contemplation of the essence of this world above, touches the eternal noumena of things, and having been nourished, laden with knowledge, it descends again to the world below." Here its spiritual experience is clothed in symbolic images which represent the work of art. In all but

This chapter is based on Florensky's *Ikonostas*, in vol. I of the YMCA Press edition, and on two other essays in the same volume (pp. 117-192 and pp. 317-352).

full correspondence with the theory of Sigmund Freud, which was popular at the beginning of this century, yet basing himself on opposite premises, Florensky concludes that "art is a solidified dream."

Fr. Pavel likewise distinguishes between two kinds of images in art. The images of *ascent* from the below to the above are "the cast-off clothing of daytime bustle, the scum of the soul, which has no place in the other world"; they are spiritually empty elements of our earthly existence. An artist is mistaken if he takes them for true revelations and wishes to fix them in his art. On the other hand, the images of *descent* are an experience of mystical life crystallized on the border between worlds. In this experience should lie the basis of true art.

Art of the ascent, to Florensky's mind, however strongly it may affect the viewer, is "an empty semblance of everyday life"—*naturalism*—which gives "a false image of reality." Whereas art of the descent—*symbolism*— "embodies otherworldly experience in real images, thus turning that which it presents into the highest reality." This art alone expresses the Truth; it is profound, *realistic*, and worthy of respect. Florensky regarded Byzantine and ancient Russian painting as such art, and within it *iconography*—"the fixing of heavenly images, the solidification on a board of the living cloud of witnesses surrounding the altar." It is for this reason that Florensky regards the icon as a proof of the existence of God. He believes that of all philosophical proofs the most convincing is the following: "There is Rublev's 'Trinity,' therefore there is God." On the other hand, he regarded western European art of the post-renaissance period as false, as art that stopped at the external shell of things and forgot about their essence. It is a naturalism occupied "only with the imitation of sensual reality, with a duplication of life, which nobody needs."

Here it is necessary to note how profoundly the final conclusions of Orthodox aesthetics, nourished by Neoplatonism and patristics as well as by the spiritual experience of Byzantine and ancient Russian artistic practice, suddenly coincided with the notions of European art following Cezanne, most fully formulated in the second decade of this century by the painter Vassily Kandinsky in his book, *On the Spiritual in Art* (1911). There is nothing surprising in this, as far as the views of Kandinsky himself are concerned, since as a spiritual being he was shaped in Russia, not without the strong influence of ancient Russian art. However, he gave equal expression to ideas of Cezannism and European symbolism which were far from the Russian icon and from Orthodoxy as a whole. What took place in the beginning of the twentieth century (and on Russian soil at that) was the fruitful encounter of Orthodox aesthetics in its final, concluding stage with the main tendency of the European artistic avant-garde—a *turning towards the spiritual in art*, the search for the most adequate, the ideal, the supra-mundane, the absolute, and so on. Western European artistic-aesthetic thinking, after having taken, since the Renaissance, the complex and not unfruitful path of serving the world below, suddenly, at the end of the nineteenth century, felt a longing for absolute spirituality and made an attempt to return to it in the theory and practice of the major representatives of the avant-garde (especially the Russians) of the early twentieth century.

But let us return to Florensky. True art, then, emerges

only when the soul, descending from the world above, is still capable of imprinting the ideas and "faces of things" it received there in symbolic images that are not merely signs. Art, in Florensky's understanding, is not at all psychological, but *ontological*; it is oriented towards a "revelation of the prototype," towards the *bringing forth* of a new, hitherto unknown reality. "The artist does not himself invent the image, but only removes the covering from an image that already exists, supramundane and eternal; he does not put paint on canvas, but, as it were, clears away the alien patina, the 'overpainting' of spiritual reality." This thought pervades the whole of Florensky's aesthetics. In another work, for example, we read: "The aim of art is the overcoming of sensual appearance, the naturalistic crust of the accidental, and the revealing of that which is stable, unchanging, and has general significance and general value in reality." Thus the symbolic image in art is itself reality, but of a higher level than the reality of the visible world. It is the icon that possesses such reality in the fullest sense.

Florensky interprets art as one of the sufficiently perfect forms of human activity, as the "closest example" to that higher activity, that "more creative art"—*theurgy*. Theurgy—"the art of God-work"—is understood by the Russian thinker as the main task of human life, "the task of the full transformation of reality by meaning, and the full actualization of meaning in reality." It was this integral human activity that constituted the basis of culture in the most ancient times. Fr. Pavel imagines it as that "ladder" down which God descends into the world and illumines matter, transfigures substance, and up which man ascends to heaven. Later culture, far from being something integral and whole, begins to disintegrate into separate activities. Theurgy is narrowed down to ritual actions and cult. Thus, art becomes one of the varieties of activity that best preserves the image and meaning of Theurgy. In it the constantly flowing and vibrant energy of the spirit finds sufficiently adequate embodiment in matter, in a thing.

To be more precise, Florensky distinguishes among three basic kinds of human activity: practical, theoretical, and liturgical (God-serving). The first produces things or "tool-machines" in a broad sense; the second produces theories, or "concept-terms"; and the third, "holy things." As for art, understood in the most general sense as "the ability to embody in matter," Fr. Pavel does not regard it as an independent activity, but understands it as a necessary aspect of any activity: theoretical, practical, or liturgical. Theoretical and liturgical activity cannot do without the art of the word, the practical and the liturgical cannot do without the visual arts, and so on. And the arts in their turn cannot do without these basic forms of activity. Therefore Florensky suggests that art be considered on a theoretical plane not as an independent activity, but "as a quality, a characteristic of the three aforementioned activities," stressing that "this quality is revealed most profoundly and vividly in the sphere of liturgics," which will be discussed in more detail in the following chapter.

Florensky's attitude to the "fine arts" proper—that is, to the arts that are non-utilitarian in the highest degree—was extremely serious, and he developed a profound theory of art which deserves to be the subject of a separate analysis. Here I will limit myself to its most general propositions.

For the author of *The Iconostasis* and a series of writings specifically on art, the work of art is an integral organism in which everything is functionally connected with everything else and there is not a single element that is useless or unnecessary to the whole. "...If there were anything accidental in it [the work—V.B.], this would testify to the fact that the work has not been fully embodied in all its parts, has not quite sprouted from the soil, and is covered in some places with lumps of dead earth," Florensky concludes in his figurative style.

The elements of a work of art do not have independent significance, but are *subject to the whole*, and their artistic significance is definable only from the viewpoint of this whole. Color, form, line, light, sound, image must be perceived and evaluated in a work of art only in their mutual interconnection and as subjected to the whole—such is Florensky's conviction. It follows that in the process of creation, the forms of all the elements that constitute the work of art must suffer a certain deformation in order to fashion in their totality the higher form of the whole work. Florensky thinks that a true work of art cannot emerge from rigid forms that are unable "to be flexible in adapting to the task of the whole." The altering of the forms of particular elements is realized in such a way that we perceive their resilience. We ought to feel the original form of an element and see how it has changed (while resisting), being affected by the force of the *whole*. Thus in a great work of art every element preserves the memory of its original form as well as the traces of the artist's creative energy.

For Florensky, a work of art is not merely a whole organism, but also a *living* organism. Once created, it goes on living in culture, long surviving its creator. It is not a dead thing, but "a never-expiring, eternally brimming stream of creativity itself," pulsing, iridescent with the colors of life, surging with the energy of the creative spirit. Here Fr. Pavel's position fully coincides with the views of Kandinsky in his book *On the Spiritual in Art*, where he speaks of the work of art as a "living being." Once separated from the artist, he says, the work acquires "an independent life, becomes a person, an independent, spiritually breathing subject, which also leads a materially real life; it becomes a being." A work of art possesses active creative powers; it lives and participates in forming the spiritual atmosphere.

However, according to Florensky, for its full-fledged life, for its "artistic being," a work of art has need of special conditions, not museum conditions as a rule, but conditions maximally close to those in which it appeared. Following the most perspicacious art critic of the beginning of the century, Pavel Muratov, he thought, for example, that Greek sculpture as an artistic phenomenon could live only under the sky of Greece, open to the sun, rain, and winds, in the atmosphere of the Greek sky, air, earth, and not in the museums of London or Berlin. And he reasoned in the same way about the icon: its real life is possible, not in a museum, but only in a functioning church.

Here Florensky posed an extremely important and still controversial problem regarding the conditions for the functioning of a work of art within culture (especially of the art of the past within the culture of subsequent epochs). Its correct solution will greatly influence the degree of effectiveness with which the spiritual potential of the art of the past can be used by present-day culture.

Florensky sees the goal of art as the transformation of reality in such a way as to reveal its essential foundations. He understands reality as "a special organization of space," and therefore perceives the main task of art as "a reorganizing of space—that is, organizing it anew, arranging it in a specific way."

From this angle of vision, the whole of culture is, for Fr. Pavel, "the activity of organizing space." When it is a case of organizing the space of our life relationships, the corresponding activity will be called technology. When it is a case of working with mental space, one can speak of scientific activity, of philosophy. "Finally, the third category of cases lies between the first two. Its space or spaces are as visual as the spaces of technology, yet, like the spaces of science and philosophy, they do not allow for living interference. The organization of such spaces is called art."

Artistic space constantly drew Florensky's attention. He sensed it deeply in every work of art; in it he perceived the foundation of the wholeness and self-worth of art. However, he saw in it not the skillful construction of the artist, not the arbitrary play of man's creative ability, but a *self-manifestation of essence* striving towards contact with the world outside itself through the mediation of the artist.

In the space of works of art, according to Florensky, was a manifestation of active "spiritual essence" in a sensually perceptible form. "The space, the space of the work of art," he writes, "this world closed in on itself, emerges into the other through its relation to the spiritual essence. Space is generated by the self-manifestation of essence; it is its light, and therefore the arrangement of space in a given work reveals the inner arrangement of its essence, is its projection and a distinct narrative about it." The multiplicity of spiritual essences that strive for self-manifestation leads to the multiplicity of forms of artistic space.

Thus art is distinguished from other kinds of activity by its special way of organizing (or re-organizing) space. All kinds of art have in common certain ways of organizing space, such as meter, rhythm, melody, visual images; but they are also distinguished one from another, first of all by principles of spatiality. In this regard, painting and graphic art can be called arts in the fullest sense of the word; poetry and music stand closer to science and philosophy; and sculpture, architecture, and theater, to technology.

In organizing artistic space, Florensky believes, music and poetry have great freedom—and music a boundless freedom. They can create whatever spaces they please, by virtue of the fact that the artist here leaves the greater part of the creative work to the listener (or reader). The poet, as a rule, gives the formula of the space, while the reader (or listener) must himself recreate the images from which the space of a given work emerges. This is a polysemous problem and a very difficult one, and the author declines responsibility in case the reader does not manage to produce vivid, integral images. The great works of Homer, Shakespeare, Dante, Goethe demand of the reader a major effort in the work of co-creation, which is far from being within the power of every man. In his consciousness the too-rich and complex spaces of the master poets' works break down into small, unconnected areas, and the artistic whole eludes his perception.

Music has still greater freedom in organizing artistic space. "Like algebra, it gives formulas that are capable of being filled with an almost infinite diversity of contents." Theater, on the other hand, presupposes considerably less activity on the part of the spectator; more rigid still are the spaces proper to architecture and sculpture. Painting and the graphic arts stand somewhere between these two extremes.

Florensky considered spatiality an extremely important principle for the classification of art, and gave special attention to it. In 1921-1924, as a professor in VHUTEMAS (the Advanced Arts and Crafts Workshops), he gave a course of lectures on "the analysis of spatiality in works of visual art." This is not the place to go into the subject in detail; but attention must be paid to the principle itself of approaching the classification of the arts from the point of view of spatiality. Thus, painting and graphic art, while belonging to the same class of spatial arrangement—that is, as opposed to music or architecture—also differ within their class according to the principle of the organization of artistic space. Graphic art, in Florensky's opinion, creates an active, moving space, and painting a passive, tactile space. The main thing in graphic art is line, which is a symbol or indicator of the direction of movement: line as the essentially abstract trace of movement. It fixes the artist's active attitude towards the world. A graphic artist affects the world, he actively gives it something of his own, and does not take from it. In fact, graphic linearity fixes the system of "effective gestures"; space in graphic art is composed of a totality of movements, or its symbols—lines.

In painting, on the other hand, space is passive to a sufficient degree. It is formed of spots, color surfaces, brushstrokes that are not symbols of action, but are themselves "certain given things which confront our sensual perception directly and wish to be taken as what they are." The color spot as a basic element in painting appears to Florensky as a gratuitous and joyful gift of the world to the artist and (through him) also to the viewer. (In this regard, the previously mentioned founder of abstractionism, Vassily Kandinsky, takes a directly opposite position.) The artist constructs painting space from color spots by means of touch, by touching the canvas with a brush dipped in paint—that is, in a tactile way, which presupposes a minimal interference in the external world ("touch is an active passivity with regard to the world"). Therefore, according to Florensky, painting space is a passive space that expresses the effect of the world upon man, and not vice versa. Aware, however, of the specific, or relative, "passivity" of this space (which is so only in view of its physical organization), he designates it by means of an antinomy: "active passivity."

"Line in graphic art is a sign or command of a certain required activity. Whereas a tangible spot is not a sign, because it does not point to a necessary activity, but itself produces a fruit gathered from the world. It is itself a certain sensual given." Painting space is passive in that it is formed by the self-sufficient, self-worthy color spot, by a certain matter that fills it. Graphic space is active because the line-movements only designate its boundaries, only give indications. In painting the major role is played by material things, or, more precisely, by *materiality*. Space here is in fact made up of things (forms, spots, strokes, and so on). The principle of materiality reigns fully, and, according to Florensky, what we have before us in a painting is in fact "not space, but a milieu": things "have diffused through the space and taken it over." However fine (light, airy) or coarse and dense this space may be, its materiality, the thing in it, is always in the forefront. Therefore the art of painting is always drawn to texture and to the use of actual objects—stickers, inlays, collage, and so on. Space in painting is inclined to turn into a milieu—that is, something consisting only of matter.

In graphic art, on the other hand, space dominates the thing. It may contain a thing, but it may also exist independently, containing nothing. Graphic art is no stranger to the notion of pure, abstract space—something that is virtually unthinkable in painting. The thing itself is understood in graphic art not as something self-worthy, but only "as a space of particular curves or fields of force."

Painting deals with matter and constructs its space following its model, and in fact following itself. Graphic art, on the contrary, is occupied first of all with the space around things, and "interprets the inside of things following its model."

Clearly, not every theorist of art (much less every artist) has precisely the same understanding of the problem of spatiality in painting and graphic art. Florensky's concept is indeed debatable, as are many other presuppositions in his aesthetics and philosophy. Nevertheless, it is profound, has inner integrity, and is logical in its own way. Art, in its particular works and also as a whole, has in principle many meanings and many aspects. Various cross sections of it are possible. That made by Florensky is fruitful as well, for it is borne out by a whole class of phenomena in the world's artistic culture.

In *The Iconostasis*, Fr. Pavel gives a different cross section of the problem of the kinds of visual art—in terms of world view and culturology. Various kinds and genres of art emerge in certain cultural and spiritual environments, expressing the "world sense" of people at the time. Thus, oil painting is a product and the fullest expression of the Roman Catholic-Renassiance world sense; engraving, in its most characteristic form, is an expression of Protestantism; and icon-painting, of Orthodox metaphysics. Without dwelling here of Florensky's culturological typology, I will note that it is far from impartial objectivism. Fr. Pavel, as a priest and an Orthodox thinker, is convinced that Orthodox culture stands closest to true culture. There is much that is true and valuable in other cultures, and he aims to support himself upon it all in his speculations, yet he sees the full-fledged ontological life of culture only in the Orthodox world. This position defines his attitude to the history of culture, and to art history in particular.

While medieval Orthodox art (Byzantine, ancient Russian) came close to revealing the metaphysical foundations of being (we will speak of this in more detail in the section entitled "The Icon"), the art of the Modern Age, beginning with the Renaissance—"renaissance" art—stopped at the external forms of the world, at naturalistic images. Florensky sees the main reason for this in the secularization of culture—its liberation from the Church and from God. The renaissance man became fascinated with the passing world, with himself, with the sensual and unstable envelope of being. He felt that worth lay in the immediate reality around him, which is only a ghostly imitation of true being. Oil painting on canvas turned out to be the most appropriate expression of the "renaissance" world sense. The sensual juiciness and materiality of the brushstroke on the elastically resilient surface of the canvas corresponded better than anything else to a portrayal of the sensually perceived, ever-changing world of man's surrounding reality. The brushstroke strives to escape the limits of the painting surface, "to enter directly into pieces of paint offered to the senses, into a colored relief, a painted statue—in short, to imitate the image, to supplant it with itself, to enter life not as a symbolic but as an empirical factor. The painted statue of a Catholic Madonna in a fashionable dress is the limit towards which the nature of oil painting gravitates," wrote Florensky.

Engraving, precisely as the realization of the very principle of graphicness, was born, according to Florensky, together with Protestantism, and is the artistic expression of its rationalistic spirit. There is also Roman Catholic engraving, but its inner gravitation is towards painting; its dense cross-hatchings are closer to the spot or brushstroke than to the line. "The true engraver's line is an abstract line; it has not only no color, but also no thickness. Contrary to the brushstroke in oils...the engraver's line wants to free itself of any taste of sensual accidents." While sensuality reigns in oil painting, the engraving is based on reason, and constructs its image out of elements that have nothing to do with elements of the visible world, on the laws of logic alone. In this sense, it is "profoundly connected with German philosophy," which grew up on Protestant soil. Without giving any further account of this interesting, though not indisputable, notion, I will emphasize that for us the important thing is the fact itself, undoubtedly correctly grasped, of the dependence between kinds and genres of art and the world sense of the social groups within which they have emerged, the spirit of the culture.

Florensky's main methodological principle in aesthetics, as in all his scientific work, is to examine the world as a whole and consider every phenomenon investigated from various points of view. He supposed that only such an approach could give the fullest and most adequate scientific image of the phenomenon under scrutiny. Thus, painting considered from the angle of spatiality and in comparison with graphic art appears as a certain element of materiality that fills its space, forms this space in the manner of a milieu, and presents itself as the only conceivable given thing. In other words, painting appears here as a self-sufficient phenomenon, which contains its entire artistic sense within itself and does not refer the viewer to anything that has being outside itself. In his essay, "Inverse Perspective," Florensky considers painting from another angle—in its relation to reality, and in comparison with the theater set. And here it reveals different facets to us. We are now talking not only of one variety of painting—easel painting in oils—but of the art of painting as a whole, as a kind of art. Whereas the theater set aims at creating a maximal imitation of reality, at supplanting or providing a full illusion of reality, painting pursues quite different aims. Its task is "not to duplicate reality, but to give the most profound understanding of its architectonics, its material, its meaning." Whereas the theater set is a beautiful deception, the "pure painting" wants to be "first of all the truth of life, which does not supplant life but only designates it symbolically in its deepest reality. The set is a screen that hides the light of being, but the pure painting is a window thrown open on reality."

The decorative painting of the stage is *illusionistic*, whereas pure painting, which is worthy in itself, has *synthetic* tasks. The theater set, which aims at creating an illusory image of reality, in fact fulfills the applied functions of theatrical art and has no independent significance. "Pure painting," on the other hand, exists at the level of high art—that is, it manifests "a new reality," "the genuine cause, life's creativity." In this consists its true *realism*, identical in this case with *symbolism* and the opposite of *naturalism*. Florensky uses the notion of realism here not in the sense of reflection, but rather in the medieval sense, as the creation of a new reality—that is, as an affirmation of the ontologism of art, which not only possesses self-worth but also points to a certain other reality. Hence the symbolism of art, and of painting in particular. In naturalism, on the other hand, according to Florensky, one finds the creating of an illusory copy of visible reality, which in fact is what the classical theater set does.

In particular, the old art of theater decoration, in striving for a maximum realization of its tasks, invented perspective—the geometrical rules for depicting three-dimensional space or volume on a plane. These rules were borrowed by painting in the "renaissance" and were maintained almost to the end of the nineteenth century. A deep analysis of the history of culture and of the data of contemporary science convinced Florensky that the vision of the world "in perspective" is by no means a natural law of normal vision, nor does it correspond to "the higher demands of pure art." Therefore, to his mind, art that constructs its works according to the academic rules of direct perspective is by no means the highest achievement in the history of art.

Here, for a correct understanding of Florensky's ideas, which are not traditional for the new European aesthetic consciousness, we must make a brief digression into his culturology. It should be remembered that his culturology emerged from the stream of the Orthodox world sense and expresses one of the directions of Orthodox thinking. To a reader brought up in a different cultural tradition, with a world view based on different principles, it may appear at least disputable, if not absurd. However, the experience of many ages of cultural history teaches us that precisely such concepts and theories often contain more truth than assertions that appear logical and indisputable to ordinary consciousness. We have no room to trace the course of Florensky's deductions even briefly. We shall limit ourselves to his main conclusions, without which his aesthetics cannot be understood.

Florensky is convinced that the history of culture is ultimately made up of two alternating and essentially different types of culture, two zones, which sometimes exist separately and sometimes (along their borders) overlap. These are *contemplative-creative* culture and *predatory-mechanical* culture. The first is characterized by an *inward* attitude towards life and a *generally human* experience of the world; the second is distinguished by an *external* attitude towards the world and *"scientific"* experience, the quintessence of which Florensky sees in the

philosophy of Kant. The first type of culture is rooted in
deep-seated, spiritual foundations of being, and it manifests itself in irrational experience. The second is oriented more towards the material world, towards the
earthly life of men, towards the laws and norms of their
existence; it is grounded in reasonable thinking, rational
schemes and mental constructs. The first type is more
ontological, the second more psychological. Florensky
considered medieval culture a characteristic example of
the first type—Orthodox culture in particular—and he
also counted many cultures of the ancient world as belonging to it, ancient Egypt, for example. The new European
culture which began with the Renaissance he considered
as belonging to the second type; late Hellenistic culture he
regarded as being of the second type as well.

To each type of culture, according to Florensky, there
corresponds a type of thinking of philosophizing—the
one *homoousian* (of one essence), the other *homoiousian*
(of similar essence). The former is primarily Christian philosophy, "*The philosophy of the idea and reason, the phi-*
losophy of the person and of creative endeavor"; it is
based on the law of personal unity, of equality with
essence. This is Orthodox philosophy par excellence, and
Russian philosophy in particular. Its originality lies precisely in its homoousian character. The philosophy of
similar essence, on the other hand, is *rationalism*—"that
is, the philosophy of the concept and reason, the philosophy
of the thing and of lifeless motionlessness...It is a fleshly
philosophy." The example here is the new philosophy of
western Europe. To be sure, both types of thinking exist in
practice only as tendencies, and not in a pure way. However, it is precisely these tendencies that distinguish Rus-

sian Orthodox from western European philosophy in the new age.

The art of one or the other type of culture has a corresponding tendency that is characteristic for the whole spirit of the culture: a striving either to *reveal the essence*, or to *create similarities*. One of the main indicators of the type of culture to which a given example of visual art belongs is *perspective. Homoiousian* painting, the creation of illusory worlds, copies of visible reality, naturalistic painting, in Fr. Pavel's terminology, cannot do without direct perspective. It rules in the "refinedly empty murals" of Pompeii, in renaissance art—"Giottism" with its secular, sensual, and even positivist spirit, with its "renaissance-like and none-too-profound vision of life"—and finally in the Russian "Wanderers" school, "a shallow phenomenon of Russian life," in Florensky's opinion, which aimed at "imitating life's surface," at "an external similarity, pragmatically useful for the most immediate actions of life."

On the other hand, *homoousian* art sets as its purpose (on the level of the collective unconscious of culture, of the inner depth of the spirit of culture) the creation not of similarities, but of "symbols of reality," not the copying of reality, but its synthesizing. It recognizes being as good, and with special attentiveness and trust examines reality, striving to comprehend the inner life of its forms and to depict them in view of their inner worth. This art proceeds not from the "scheme of Euclidean-Kantian space" artificially applied by reason to real space, but from the more complex laws of its real organization. As examples of such art Florensky cites the art of ancient Egypt, of classical Greece, of the European middle ages, of ancient Russia, and, to some extent, the budding new art of the twentieth century.

He believed that the art of these cultures did not apply the rules of direct perspective, not because it was unaware of them, but because they did not correspond to the type of these cultures, to the type of thinking of its bearers, or, finally, to the "artistic method" (Florensky's term) characteristic of these cultures. Their methods of portrayal were based on a non-euclidian understanding of space and, accordingly, on special means of representation, in particular the applying of "inverse perspective," which, as Florensky supposed, is more characteristic of human psycho-physiology than direct perspective. It is no accident that children begin by portraying space in inverse perspective—something their parents and teachers try actively to correct in them. This, Fr. Pavel supposes, is also what happened in the history of culture since the time of the Renaissance, when, with the secularization of culture and the domination of rationalism, there began a "forced re-education" of human psycho-physiology "in the direction of the abstract demands of the new world view, which was essentially anti-artistic, which essentially excluded art from itself, visual art in particular." On the basis of a fundamental study of art history, as well as of the data of psycho-physiology and other sciences from the beginning of this century, Florensky came to the conclusion that "the perspective picture of the world is not a fact of perception, but merely a demand made in the name of some perhaps very strong, but decidedly abstract, considerations." "Perspectivity" is not a property of the real world or of human perception. In Florensky's opinion, it is one of many possible methods of "symbolic expression," and is by no means universal or superior to other methods. Moreover, the "perspective" method of portraying the world is "an extremely narrow method, extremely cramped, restricted by a multitude of additional conditions."

The method of medieval art, on the other hand, in principle ignoring direct perspective, opens up wide possibilities for artistic creativity. "The artist portrays not the thing, but the life of the thing according to his impression of it." This means that the representation is not a momentary photograph of the thing, but a certain *synthetic image* of it which emerges in the process of its comprehensive examination. Living perception—it is precisely this that constitutes the life of such a synthetic image, ever changing, pulsating, sparkling, turning its various facets to the light of the spiritual vision. The artist takes from this image, which lives in his spiritual world, "that which is most vivid, most expressive, and instead of a more or less enduring display of psychic fireworks, gives a motionless mosaic of its separate and most striking moments." This "mosaic" image certainly has nothing in common with the illusionist picture fixed by one unmoving eye located at a definite point in space, as the rules of direct perspective require. The eye of the viewer, as he contemplates the painting, glides over the portrayed "mosaic" of the synthetic image and, like a needle running on a phonograph record, "reads" the image, invoking responsive vibrations in the viewer's soul. "It is these vibrations that make up the goal of the work of art."

Fr. Pavel's views of the goal of the work of art were characteristic of Russian culture in the early twentieth century. They coincide almost completely, for example, with the understanding of Vassily Kandinsky, who wrote at that time, in his book *On the Spiritual in Art*, that painting enriches man spiritually by exciting special "vibrations of the soul" in him. The artist is guided in his activity by one thing only—"the principle of inner necessity" which unconsciously governs the organizing of harmonious forms on canvas, with the aim of "purposefully touching the human soul." Close to this was the understanding of many other founders of the new art, which, starting with Cezanne and Gauguin, strove as did medieval art to get away from portraying the visible forms of reality and towards an artistic expression of *the essential foundations of being* as a whole and of its particular phenomena, towards *bringing out the inner resonance* of each thing, towards a regeneration of the spiritual potential of artistic work.

Florensky, standing at the beginning of the century, felt strongly the coming of an essentially new stage in culture and art, a stage that would break with the traditions of the preceding culture of the Modern Age, and would establish invisible bonds, "invisible nerves and arteries," with medieval culture, drawing spiritual nourishment from it. "The new Middle Ages are at hand," he wrote in his article, "Forebears of the Love of Wisdom."*

* Florensky's article "Forbears of the Love of Wisdom" (*Prashchury lyubomudria*) was published in *Bogoslovsky Vestnik*, vol. 1, no. 4 (1910), pp. 614-644.

4

Cult

The overcoming of the boundary between the earthly and the heavenly, in Florensky's conviction, is realized not only on the paths of individual creativity (mystical or artistic), but also with the help of *a catholic entry through cult.*

The philosophy of cult is the most important, if not the main, part of Pavel Florensky's spiritual legacy. There is no room here to speak of it in detail, but without referring to it, a correct grasp of his aesthetics is impossible. In Florensky's understanding, cult, which constitutes the foundation of culture, is the place of encounter of the two worlds; it is "that part of reality, set aside from all the rest, where the immanent and the transcendent, that which is below and that which is above, the here and the there, the temporal and the eternal, the conditional and the unconditional, the corruptible and the incorruptible all meet." The spiritual nucleus of cult, its focal point, is the worship of God, around which other activities cluster, accompanying it or separating from it completely, forming human culture as a whole. Artistic

This chapter is based on Florensky's cycle of lectures on "Cult and Culture" published in *Bogoslovskie Trudy*, vol. XVII (Moscow, 1977), pp. 87-248 (one lecture from which was published in English translation under the title "Mysteries and Rites" in St *Vladimir's Theological Quarterly,* vol. 30, no. 4), as well as on *Ikonostas* and "Memoirs of Childhood, Religion, Nature," both cited above.

activity exists outside of worship as well as within it, though the second case, in Florensky's view, undoubtedly has higher significance.

Worship, according to Florensky, is "the flower of Church life" and, moreover, "the heart of the Church's life," for in it, as in some cosmic focus, all that is divine and all that is human are concentrated, its main content being *Humanity*. The purpose of cult is to *transform* the natural, the human, the accidental into the sacred, the harmonious, the objective, the ideal. It is to help man give fullest *expression* to the emotions (joy, grief, regret) and the passions that fill him. Cult fulfills an important aesthetico-ontological task in culture. "It affirms the whole of human nature, with all its affects," Fr. Pavel writes; "it allows every affect its greatest possible scope, opening for it the boundless freedom of release, leading it to a beneficial crisis, and thereby purifying and healing the τραύματα τῆς ψυχῆς [the traumas of the soul—V.B.]. Cult in fact leads man to *catharsis*.

Florensky quotes from a poem (a "slightly silly" poem, as he puts it) by Konstantin Balmont:

>It is not enough to cry, we need
>Orderly, harmonious weeping.
>One must act calmly to create
>A beautiful countenance.
>Sincere suffering is not enough,
>You are not alone in the world.

And he comments: "As I say, the expression is somewhat mincing, somewhat self-conscious, and yet he is right. 'We need orderly, harmonious weeping,' because we must transform life, the whole of life, in all its manifestations, into harmony. Is it not in this that culture consists? That humanity consists?"

However, man in his solitude, in his grief, in his alienation and "helpless subjectivity" is of course unable to rise on his own to "harmonious weeping," to an ideal expression of the state of his inner world. It is here that he is helped by worship, by the Church's cult, which "prompts such weeping as we would never be able to invent for ourselves—so adequate to *each one* of us, our personal weeping. Cult weeps with us for us, it speaks words which are exactly what we would want to say but would never be able to say. In short, to our dim individual grief, to our chaotic, accidentally shaped, and, perhaps, in our own minds, even illicit grief, it gives universal form, the form of pure humanity. Cult raises grief in us, and thereby it raises us in our grief, to the level of ideal humanity, to that very human nature created in the likeness of Christ, and thus transfers our grief to Pure Humanity, to the Son of Man. It unburdens us as individuals, if frees, heals, lightens us." In cult our personal grief (or other feeling) is lightened and raised to an objective, universal state; it becomes an impulse of life, which urges us to strive towards true humanity. Our ordinary transient life is sanctified by cult. "Then we may wonder whether we have not received more than we lost, whether we are not rewarded a hundredfold: for the well-springs of the sweetest tears and the most fragrant words are opened."

Cult, according to Florensky, is a special and perhaps the chief activity of man, because it is oriented towards uniting two artificially separated worlds—the heavenly and the earthly, the spiritual and the material; it is the activity of "joining meaning and reality together." As the result of such activity, which unites all people into one catholic mankind, each participant has the real possibility of escaping "subjective self-containedness" and acquiring support "in absolute, objective reality"—that is, of finding his concrete place in the universe, which is assigned only to him, of feeling himself an equal among equals, a son, not a stepson, of the divine Father.

Orthodox worship, embodying the tradition of "mental prayer" or "mental endeavor," is not an invention of the human intellect; it has descended to us from the "reasonable Heavenly Powers," and this is why every man's "mute and wingless anxiety of soul" acquires ideal expression in it, "finds its word and flies off to the world of highest satisfaction."

Worship has an external ritual side and an inner sacral side. In church ritual, the spiritual content of cult, invisible and intangible in itself, acquires flesh, an external expression; the mystery which Florensky briefly defines as *the holy* is embodied in ritual. Holiness—this is that general human value which the Church gives to the world in various forms of expression, particularly in sacraments, worship, icons. In a cultic action, in a ritual, holiness fills "bits of the ordinary, snippets of life taken from the ordinary" with new content, it lights them up, it makes them qualitatively different from what they were in ordinary life.

The bearers of holiness in the Church's cult are not only the sacraments and the clergy, but also objects, "the tools of cult—icons, cross, chalice, paten, censer, vestments, and so on." They are at the same time both material things and "inner senses," "spiritual values," "holy things." They are antinomic in essence, a uniting of the un-unitable—of "the temporal and the eternal, value and accident, the incorruptible and the perishing." In short, they are *symbols*.

We have already pointed out more than once that for Florensky the most profound and true art is *symbolic* art, as opposed to naturalistic art, which copies the external appearance of reality. (In the broadest sense, however, he regarded all art as symbolic, and the symbolic or naturalistic alone, in a pure state, as altogether impossible.) For him the model of symbolism in art was the icon. But artistic symbols are only one class of symbols in Fr. Pavel's theory. He first gives a more general understanding of the symbol in connection with cult symbols, and then goes on to other sorts and kinds of symbols.

In his memoirs, Florensky wrote that everything symbolic, as belonging to the category of the *particular*, the unusual, had excited him from early childhood and drawn the attention of his searching mind. "All my life," he wrote, "I have thought about only one problem—the problem of the symbol." He saw in it a material incarnation of the spiritual—that is, in a certain sense, a focus of creation—for, as he himself emphasized, he never thought of the spiritual abstractly, out of touch with the phenomenon. "I wanted to see the soul," he wrote, "but I wanted to see it embodied," meaning in a certain "spiritually-material" concretion or symbol. It was in this sense that Florensky considered himself a symbolist.

The spiritual, according to Fr. Pavel, expresses itself only in matter. Therefore, sensually received symbols do not conceal or obscure "spiritual essences" but, on the contrary, reveal them. Since childhood Florensky had seen the "translucence" of the other world through symbols, and by this his soul and his inquiring mind were forever drawn to them. "For the mystery of the world is not hidden, but is precisely revealed through symbols in its true essence—that is, as a mystery. A beautiful body is not concealed but revealed by clothing, and revealed as more beautiful, for it is revealed in its chaste modesty."

Florensky understands the symbol not just as a purely semiotic unity, but also as an ontologial unity; it not only signifies something other, but itself is the bearer of this other, "the living, mutual penetration of two beings"; it is bi-une in nature. Two worlds are united in the symbol—the one to which the symbol belongs materially, and the one to which it points, whose signifier it is. The symbol has an inner connection with that which it symbolizes; it is endowed, if only partially, with the spiritual power of the signified. Therefore it does not simply signify, but also *really manifests the signified.*

Florensky expanded into a general understanding of the symbol the concept of the *liturgical symbol* or *image*, well known in later patristic writings, a concept which Byzantine commentators on the liturgy as a rule referred only to cult symbols. For the Byzantines, these were bearers of the energy of the archetype, and in this they saw their holiness. Fr. Pavel took this concept to its logical conclusion, ascribing the presence of the spiritual power of the archetype to the nature of the symbol in general—that is, expanding the limits of liturgical symbolism to include all symbolism.

Interestingly, this understanding, or rather intuition, of the nature of the symbol was born in Florensky not only long before he had any substantial acquaintance with the patristic theory of the symbol, or with Orthodoxy in general, but even, it seems, in his very early childhood. His parents deliberately raised their children without religion; they baptized them, as was customary, but never took them to church or spoke with them about religious subjects. For a long time Florensky "did not even know how to cross himself." So that as far as the future theologian's early liturgical experience is concerned, there is nothing to speak of. More interesting still is one of his early experiences, recorded in 1916. Some relatives once brought some wonderful grapes to Florensky's house. Young Pavel was given only a few to try, for fear they might upset his stomach, and to stop the boy from nagging his parents, his father drew a monkey on a big sheet of paper, placed the drawing behind the grapes, and said that the monkey would not allow him to have any more. The image affected the little boy, Florensky recalls, far more strongly than a live monkey would have done. He sensed in it certain mystical forces of nature, more powerful than nature itself. It was then, he writes, that "I acquired the basic thought of my world view: that what is named in the name, what is symbolized in the symbol, the reality of what is pictured in the picture, is indeed present, and therefore the symbol *is* the symbolized."

In the young Pavel's unconscious a remnant of the most ancient sacral consciousness had been preserved, apparently going back to the time when the first primitive humans appeared. Among later cultures this type of symbolic consciousness was especially characteristic of the ancient Egyptians and the Israelites. For the ancient Jews, the name was the bearer of the essence, and therefore the name of God, especially, could not be pronounced; even to this day we do not know how it was pronounced, though the spelling has been preserved. This understanding of the symbol was inherited from the near-eastern peoples by Christianity, and has remained in Orthodoxy into the twentieth century.

In his essay, "Onomadoxy as a Philosophical Premise,"* Florensky gives one of his most capacious definitions of the symbol, one also showing its bi-une nature: "A being that is greater than itself—this is the basic definition of the symbol. A symbol is something that manifests in itself that which is not itself, that which is greater than itself and is nevertheless essentially manifested through itself...a symbol is an essence the energy of which is joined, or, more precisely, commingled, with the energy of another essence, more worthy in a given respect, and which thereby carries this other essence in itself."

The symbol, according to Florensky, is antinomic in principle, meaning that it unites things which are mutually exclusive from the point of view of one-dimensional, formally logical thinking. Therefore a man of the new European culture has difficulty comprehending its nature. However, the symbol did not present any difficulty for the thinking of ancient peoples, of which it was often the basic element. The embodiments of nature in folk poetry and in ancient poetry, which are now perceived as metaphors, are not metaphors at all in Florensky's judgment; they are precisely symbols in the above-mentioned sense, not "stylistic embellishments and seasonings," not rhetorical figures. "...For an ancient poet, the life of the elements was not a stylistic phenomenon, but a matter-of-fact expression of essence." For a modern poet, it is only

* Florensky's essay *Imeslavie kak philosophskaya predposylka* ("Onomadoxy as a Philosophical Premise") was published in the collection *Materialy k sporu o pochitanii Imeni Bozhiya* ("Materials on the controversy over the veneration of the Name of God"), Moscow, 1913.

in moments of special inspiration that "these deepest layers of spiritual life break through the crust of the alien world view of our modern age, and he can speak in intelligible language of what has become unintelligible to us—the life of our own soul, along with the whole of creation."

The symbol, in Fr. Pavel's understanding, has "two thresholds of receptivity," an upper and a lower, within which it still remains a symbol. The upper threshold preserves the symbol from "the exaggeration of the natural mysticism of matter," from "naturalism," in which the symbol is wholly identified with the archetype. This extremity was characteristic of ancient times. The Modern Age tends to go beyond the lower limit, in which case the material connection between symbol and archetype is broken, their common matter is ignored, and energy and symbol are perceived only as signs of the archetype, not as its energetico-material bearer.

The symbol is "an outer manifestation of the hidden essence," a revelation of the essence itself, its "embodiment in the outside environment." Precisely in this way, for example, in sacral and secular symbolism, clothing symbolizes the body. Florensky gives close attention to symbols, especially to specific cultic symbols, in many of his works. In particular, precisely in the context of symbolic thinking, he compares the sacraments with one of the most significant symbols of ancient culture—the mirror. "The sacraments are greater and more profound than the mirror, of course; but we ought not to belittle the mirror reflection, for it reveals to us not a semblance of reality, but reality itself, in the original, though it does so instrumentally." We must bear this thought in mind, as well as Florensky's general understanding of the symbol, when we become acquainted with his concept of the icon.

Cultic rituals—divine services—are organized according to a system including a whole series of arts, which Florensky calls "Church art" and takes to be "the highest synthesis of heterogeneous artistic activities." Architecture, painting, the applied-decorative and musical-poetic arts, the choreography of the clergy, the visual (color and light) and olfactory (incense) atmosphere of the church, all participate in this synthesis. According to Florensky, each kind of Church art was created with an eye to its functioning in a system along with other kinds, and can be correctly perceived and understood only within the process of this functioning—that is, within the process of Church ritual.

In particular, such peculiarities of icons as "the exaggeration of certain proportions, the emphasizing of lines, the abundance of gold and precious stones, settings and crowns, pendants and covers—of brocade, velvet, embroidered with pearls and gems—all this lives in conditions peculiar to the icon, not at all as a piquant exoticism, but as the necessary, irremoveable, and only way of expressing the spiritual content of the icon; that is, as a unity of style and content, or, in other words, as true artistry." Precisely for this reason, Florensky is categorically opposed to the exhibiting of icons in museums. He believes that away from the church atmosphere, away from the warm, broken, colorful, flickering light of many candles and icon lamps, they are only "caricatures" of icons; whereas in a church, and "face to face" with the one who contemplates them, they reveal "the world of platonic ideas."

In the church synthesis, Florensky thinks, "everything is intertwined with everything else." Even such an apparently insignificant element as the "ribbons of bluish incense smoke" waving around the pillars and over the frescoes plays an important role in the system of the ritual. By their movement the streams of incense "almost infinitely expand the architectural space of the church, soften the dryness and rigidity of its lines, and, as if melting them, imbue them with movement and life." Organically united with this plasticity and with the rhythmic movements of the clergy, the play and gleaming of light on the folds of precious fabrics, the incense, the "special fiery breathing of the atmosphere," the vocal and poetic arts merge on the aesthetic level into an integral musical drama. "Here everything is subjected to one purpose, the crowning cathartic effect of this musical drama."

The complex church ritual of Orthodox cult, which took shape over the course of many centuries, was finally interpreted in Florensky's work not only in its sacral-liturgical aspect, but also as an aesthetic phenomenon, though many Byzantine commentators on the liturgy had already made tentative approaches to such an interpretation. Fr. Pavel summarized them on the basis of the artistic-aesthetic and spiritual experience of his time and gave them a logical conclusion. He interpreted the artistic-aesthetic aspect of Church art as an effective means of raising the participants in worship from the world below to the world above.

The worship of God takes place in a church which Florensky understands as in all respects the fulfillment of Orthodox tradition, as a symbol and means of "ascending on high." The very structure of architectural space in a church is directed from external to internal, from material to spiritual, from earth to heaven, which is within, in the nucleus of the church. It is the sanctuary with its contents. "The spatial nucleus of he church is indicated by its coverings: courtyard, vestibule, the church proper, the sanctuary, the altar, the antimension, the chalice, the Holy Gifts, Christ, the Father." The whole of the sanctuary in the church is "a space not of this world," a spiritual heaven with all its inhabitants in the full and direct sense of the word. The border between the sanctuary and the church, heaven and earth, is formed of the "visible witnesses of the invisible world," the living symbols of the unity of the two worlds, living beings who in popular parlance have long been known as "angels in the flesh." They surround the sanctuary and, like "living stones," form the wall of the iconostasis.

Florensky understands the iconostasis in its true meaning not as boards, stone, and brick, but as a *living wall of witnesses* who stand around the throne of God and announce the mystery to all who pray in the church. "The iconostasis is a vision. The iconostasis is a manifestation of the saints and the angels—an angelophany, the manifestation of the heavenly witnesses, first of all the Mother of God and Christ Himself in the flesh—witnesses announcing what is on the other side of the flesh. The iconostasis is the saints themselves." If all the faithful in the church possessed spiritual vision, they would always see this row of witnesses of "His awesome and glorious presence" and there would be no need for any other iconostasis. Unfortunately, this is not so, and because of the infirm spiritual vision of the faithful, the Church is forced to create "a certain aid for spiritual sluggishness," a sort of "crutch for spirituality"—a material iconostasis, a wall with icons on which heavenly visions are fixed materially, "bound in paint."

Without the iconostasis, for the spiritually blind the sanctuary would be closed off by a "blank wall." The iconostasis makes "windows" in it, through which one can see what takes place beyond it—"the living witnesses of God." Hence, the basic purpose of icons as the main element of the iconostasis is to serve as windows onto the other world. On this basis, Fr. Pavel builds his whole theology and aesthetics of the icon.

5

The Icon

The philosophy of the icon, which had been shaped over centuries in the cultures of Byzantium and ancient Russia, found its fullest expression in the work of Pavel Florensky. It still awaits special study. Here I wish only to point to certain basic propositions in the context of Florensky's aesthetic system.

One can see from what has already been said that for Florensky the icon is the highest kind of pictorial art, and perhaps of art in general. Its place in the church and its role in worship are unique; no less is its significance in ordinary life. Reflecting of icons from the cell of St Sergius of Radonezh, Fr. Pavel emphasizes that in the fourteenth century an icon was not merely a bit of decor, part of the "furnishings of a room, as it is now, but was the vivifying soul of the house, its spiritual center, a mentally conceivable axis around which the whole house turned." A prayer icon was carefully chosen in correspondence with the owner's spiritual cast, and therefore was in fact the "spiritual mold" of its owner, "the very witness of his inner life." The character of the icons Sergius of Radonezh chose for his private prayer allows us "to understand the constitution of his own spirit," his "inner life," the spiritual forces on which the "father of Russia" nourished himself.

This chapter is based on *Ikonostas* and other articles on aesthetics published in vol. I of the YMCA Press edition.

Continuing the platonic-patristic tradition, Florensky believes that "the icon is a reminder of the archetype on high." A man does not receive knowledge from outside through contemplating an icon, but evokes in himself the memory of the forgotten depth of being, of his spiritual homeland, and this remembrance brings him the joy of recovering the forgotten truth. The icon, however, contains only a scheme, a sensually perceived "reconstruction" of spiritual experience, of the invisible world, of "mental reality." It presents visually "that which is not given to sensual experience." However, such a "reconstruction" has a particular, specific character—it is a reconstruction at once aesthetic and sacral.

The icon, for Florensky, is "speculation in visual images," "an aesthetic phenomenon," "the highest kind of art," located at the summit of artistic-aesthetic values. The aesthetic here is understood, not in the sense of Baumgarten's aesthetics, but in that deeply mystical meaning which for centuries was taking shape in Orthodox culture, was consolidated in the collections of "Philokalia," and was formulated by Florensky as applied above all to asceticism.

According to this understanding, the icon, while it is an aesthetic phenomenon, is not limited to the artistic sphere alone, but exceeds its limits significantly. The icon, Florensky wrote, "is not a work of art, a product of self-sufficient creativity, but a work of witness, which has need of art along with many other things." By this he strives to warn his readers against a purely artistic, aestheticizing approach to the icon, which confines itself to the icon's pictorially expressive aspects (however high their level!).

True painting, he thought, is something more than a mere pictorial surface. It "has as its goal to bring the viewer beyond the limits of sensually perceived paint and canvas into a certain reality, and then the pictorial work shares the basic ontological character of all symbols generally, that of *being what they symbolize.*" Here the most important principle of religious, and precisely of Orthodox, aesthetics is formulated. Art, as we know, does not claim to be anything else but essentially a work of art either in platonism or in the western European idealistic aesthetics rooted in platonism, much less in materialism. And this does not exclude, but rather defines its function as sign and symbol, its artistic-aesthetic worth. Orthodox aesthetics has always regarded this as insufficient.

Since patristic times its theoreticians have perceived in the icon a charismatic function, among many others; that is, they have seen it as a bearer of the energy (and grace) of the archetype it portrays. Hence the widespread Orthodox belief in miracle-working icons. Fr. Pavel brings these ideas to their logical conclusion.

He reminds us that the icon originated historically from the mask—the ancient Egyptian funerary mask—and that it basically preserved its functions, though in a new way, transformed through the process of cultural creativity. Florensky also traces the historical development of the mask into the icon. It first existed as a painting on the inner wooden sarcophagus, then as the Hellenistic funerary portrait on wood (now known to art history as the Fayum portrait). Florensky explains the illusionism of these portraits as "a leftover from the former sculpted surface of the sarcophagus," as "a painted equivalent" of a three-dimensional sculpture. The next step, finally, was to the Christian icon, which also emerged in Egypt, and initially bore a strong resemblance to "Hellenistic portraiture."

Florensky sees a metaphysical relation between the Egyptian funerary mask and the Christian icon. In the funerary cult, the mask was perceived not as a portrait but as a *manifestation* of the deceased in his new heavenly condition, as a manifestation of the spiritual energy of the deceased, a manifestation of the person himself. Egyptian Christians preserved the same "ontology": "For them, too, the icon of a witness was not a portrait, but the witness himself, who witnessed by it and through it." This awareness of the ontological connection between an icon and the body of the saint has always been preserved in Orthodoxy.

For a believer, the reality of this connection lies in the foundation of his faith. The icon not only raises him up mentally to the archetype, it stands as a symbol in the sense mentioned earlier—that is, it reveals the archetype to him and brings his consciousness in reality to the spiritual world, showing him "hidden and supernatural sights." An iconographer, Florensky insists, does not create an image; he does not invent, does not paint a portrait. With his brush he simply lifts the scales that cover our spiritual vision; he parts the curtains (or opens the window) beyond which the original stands. "Now I look at the icon," Florensky writes, "and I say to myself: 'Behold, this is She—not her picture but She Herself, contemplated by means of, with the aid of, iconographic art. As through a window, I see the Mother of God...'"

In Orthodoxy, spiritual ontology in its deepest foundations is on principle inaccessible to human reason. Fr.

Pavel is well aware of that, and he does not strive for an ultimate ontological understanding of the icon *as a real manifestation of the essence*. What is important for him is to convince his contemporaries, infected by positivism, that they should "by no means get stuck on its [the icon's—V.B..] psychological, associative meaning, that is, its meaning as a picture." An icon is first of all a *symbol*, which in Florensky's understanding is always ontologically inseparable from its archetype, being, as it were, its "leading wave," its manifestation, energy, light. It was precisely in this ontological sense that icons were understood by the icon-venerators during the period of Byzantine iconoclasm.

Orthodox consciousness has always regarded the icon as "a certain fact of divine reality." "A true spiritual experience," "a true perception of the other-worldly," always lies at its foundation. When this experience is sealed in an icon for the first time, it is regarded as a "first-revealed" or "prototypal" icon. Copies may be made of it that are externally more or less close, and that are done with more or less skill. However, their "spiritual content" will not depend on their form or skill. It is not similar but *the same* in all of them as in the original, even when it shows through "dull coverings and dim media." It is this that constitutes the ontological and sacral meaning of the icon.

This meaning also basically defines the icon's artistic and pictorial order—essentially the specifics peculiar to the icon, which make it unlike anything else. Florensky believes that iconography, in contrast to painting and graphic art, is "a concrete metaphysics of being." "Whereas oil painting is most fit for conveying the sensual data of the world, and engraving its mental scheme, the icon exists as a visual manifestation of the metaphysical essence of what it depicts." It is precisely the need to express the concrete metaphysics of the world that defines the basic methods of iconography.

Iconography is not interested in anything accidental; its subject is the true nature of things, the "God-created world in its trans-worldly beauty." Therefore an iconographic depiction does not (must not) contain any accidental elements. The whole of it, in all its details and minutiae, is an image of the archetypal world—"of lofty, heavenly essences." The icon, according to Florensky, is a unified artistic organism. The whole metaphysical essence concretely manifested in an icon also defines the icon's integrity, to which all pictorial means are subordinated. The icon, finally, is "an image of the world to come"; it enables us to "leap over time" and see images of the future which are "thoroughly concrete." It is therefore meaningless to speak of some of its elements being accidental.

Of course, Fr. Pavel has in mind not specific examples of iconography, but first of all the icon in its essence, the ideal icon. Specific icons may occasionally contain accidental and unnecessary elements, but these do not define their essence. "What is accidental in an icon is not accidental to the icon." It comes from either inexperience or want of skill in the artist, or from his marked artistic individuality.

The latter is essential for painters of a post-renaissance orientation. A marked artistic individuality is the most important indication of value in works of the Renaissance cultural type. In iconography, on the contrary, as characteristic of the medieval cultural type, individuality leads to the appearance of numerous accidental elements which obscure the truth. The workshop production of icons, when several masters work on a single image, helps to avoid this problem. Mutually correcting each other in their "inadvertent departures from objectivity" by working in a catholic way [*soborno*], they achieve what is the main thing for iconography—"the uncloudedness of catholically transmitted truth."

What served as the criterion of this "uncloudedness"? What guided iconographers in their activity of "opening windows" onto the world above? According to Florensky, the criteria were *spiritual experience* and *iconographic canons.*

The author of *Iconostasis* thought that in the most direct and precise sense only saints could be iconographers, for to them alone are disclosed the heavenly visions that should be embodied in an icon. However, only certain iconographers over many centuries of iconography have possessed the spiritual experience of saints, their number, according to Christian tradition, being headed by the apostle Luke. More often they were guided by the experience of holy fathers who lacked the gift for iconography. Therefore Florensky, following an Orthodox tradition that goes back to the Seventh Ecumenical Council, regards as the true creators of icons those holy fathers who "with their spiritual experience directed the hands of iconographers who were sufficiently experienced in technique to be able to embody heavenly visions and sufficiently educated to be sensitive to the suggestions of a blessed mentor." Given the general catholic spirit of medieval culture and the "cohesion of medieval consciousness," such a creative union contributed, in Florensky's opinion, to the most perfect organizing of iconography.

Not all craftsmen were able to work together with a saint. But iconographers, to whom Florensky gives the respectful title of "technicians of the brush," were not so far from spirituality as to be unaware of the loftiness and holiness of the deed they were undertaking. Therefore, in the Church, they occupy a place intermediate between the servants of the altar and simple laymen. In ancient times, outstanding masters of iconography were called philosophers. Though they might not have written a single word in the theoretical sense, they "bore witness to the incarnate Word with the fingers of their hands, and truly philosophized in color." Thus they were the equals of theologians, since in ancient times the "witness of the spiritual world" was called philosophy regardless of the form in which it was realized.

Florensky divides icons into four categories, depending on the source from which they arose, that is, on the character of the spiritual experience that lay at their basis: (1) biblical icons, based on the reality given by the word of God; (2) portrait icons, based on the iconographer's own experience and memory, if he was a participant in or contemporary of the events or persons depicted; (3) icons painted on the basis of tradition, that is, using the spiritual experience of others, conveyed to the iconographer orally or in writing; and (4) "revealed" icons, based on the iconographer's own spiritual experience, on the spiritual reality revealed to him in a vision or dream. Icons of the first three categories may also be regarded as "revealed" in a sense, because they are based on "a certain vision" of the iconographer's, without which the visual image would be unthinkable.

Florensky regarded the "Trinity" of Andrey Rublev as revealed and "previously unknown to the world." Its basis, he thought, was in the spiritual experience of Sergius of Radonezh, from whom Rublev received "a new vision of the world." He was therefore inclined to see Rublev as an executor of genius, while he considered the true creator of "the greatest work not only of Russian but of all world art" to be St Sergius himself.

The iconography of the three angels at Abraham's table goes back to deep antiquity. But these were all icons illustrating the biblical event—the appearance of the three sojourners to Abraham—though they had also long been regarded as symbolizing the Trinity. In Rublev's icon, however, Florensky sees a qualitatively new stage in the revelation—the appearance of the Trinity itself in its main aspect, that of all-embracing love. In Rublev's icon we are struck and "burned...by the sudden tearing away of the curtain of the noumenal world before our eyes. On the aesthetic level, what is important for us is not how the iconographer achieved this baring of the noumenal...but that he truly conveyed to us the revelation he beheld." Rublev, in embodying Sergius's experience, opened to the spiritual eyes of the viewer the very essence of "inexhaustible, infinite love." "To the enmity and hatred reigning below there is opposed this mutual love, flowing in eternal harmony, in eternal silent conversation, in the eternal unity of the lofty spheres."

Florensky regarded the "Trinity," and after it and along with it Russian iconography of the fourteenth and fifteenth centuries, as the summit of pictorial art "unique in world history"—as "the perfection of the pictorial," to which he could find no equal in the history of the world's art. He considered only classical Greek sculpture comparable to it in a certain sense. In the Russian icon "visions of pristine purity" attained the clearest forms of expression, "all-human truths" received the most adequate forms of artistic embodiment. What was faintly discernible in the Zeus, Athena, or Isis of antiquity found its "universally human" forms in the Christ Pantokrator and the Mother of God of Russian iconography in the fourteenth and fifteenth centuries.

However, beginning with the end of the sixteenth century, along with the impoverishment of Church life, there were also signs of a "reduction" of iconography. It lost its depth of penetration into the spiritual world and, trying to conceal its spiritual blindness, replaced those universal ontological symbols, which had become incomprehensible, with complex allegories addressed only to superficial reason and theological erudition. With the loss of spiritual experience, iconography also lost its ability to create icons in the proper sense of the word.

Thus the spiritual experience of the iconographers themselves, or of the holy fathers, was the basis of iconography and the criterion of true icons. However, icon painters did not always have holy fathers "at hand." Therefore, in the process of the historical existence of Church art, the visual-spiritual experience pertaining to iconography was consolidated into an iconographic canon, which Florensky sees as the spiritual prescription of holy fathers to the "technicians of the brush."

Polemicizing with the experience of the new European art as a whole, including contemporary art and art theory, Florensky insists that norms and canons are always necessary for true artistic work. In canons mankind's spiritual experience over many centuries is consolidated, and by working within their framework the artist is united with that experience. "Difficult canonical forms in all areas of art have always been a touchstone on which nonentities are broken and true talents are sharpened. Bringing the artist's creative energy to the heights achieved by mankind, canonic form frees it for new achievements, for creative flight; it also frees him from the necessity of repeating elementary steps: what canonical form demands, or, more precisely, what mankind gives to the artist in canonical form, is freedom and not constraint." Here Fr. Pavel formulates the main principle by which Orthodox art has been guided, to a greater or lesser degree, in the course of its entire history (in Byzantium as well as in Slavic countries). The departure from the principle of canonicity that began to appear in Russian church art in the seventeenth century put Florensky on the alert. Addressing his contemporaries—the artists Vrubel, Vasnetsov, Nesterov, and other new icon-painters, who created such a quantity of new icons as Church history had never known—he asks: are you sure you have told the truth in them? The author of *Iconostasis* had no such assurance.

In the end, Florensky declares, the Church has little interest in form. The main thing for her is the truth she demands of art. And in this sense "the Church's understanding of art was, is, and will always be one thing—realism," meaning a real manifestation of the truth. And the truth, as has already been shown, is far from being revealed to everyone. In the course of history, mankind has gathered it up bit by bit, and has fixed this experience of collective knowledge, or "the condensed reason of mankind," in artistic canons. The true artist, Florensky believes, does not strive for subjective self-expression, for perpetuating his individuality, but desires "the beautiful, the objectively beautiful, that is, the artistically embodied truth," and on this path the canons render him an invaluable service. Canonical form in iconography "is the form of the greatest naturalness" for expressing the deepest spiritual experience of universally human truths.

According to Florensky, the medieval artist, as distinct from the new European artist, was not troubled by whether he was the first or the hundredth to speak the truth. For him, it was important not to deviate from it, to express it, and thereby secure the value of his work. And this truth is expressed with greatest fullness in "universally human" artistic canons. Therefore the artist, in understanding and following them, acquires the ability "to embody a truly contemplated reality." His personal spiritual experience is in this case supported and strengthened by the experience of preceding generations. The artist who does not follow the canons turns out to be inferior to the level of the artistic embodiment of truth attained over time. What is personal, individual in him, becomes accidental, far removed from the real spiritual achievements of mankind.

At the same time, the canons by no means constrain the iconographer's creative possibilities, as becomes obvious when one compares a series of old of icons "of the same canonical pattern: you will find no two that are identical to each other." In the canons, the "universally human" truth is embodied with the greatest fullness, naturalness, and simplicity. The artist who has mastered them "breathes freely within the canonical forms: they unaccustom him to the accidental, which is a hindrance to movement. The more stable and firm the canon is, the more deeply and purely it expresses a generally human spiritual need: the canonical is the churchly, the churchly is the catholic, and the catholic is the universally human." This religious and aesthetic creed lay at the basis of all artistic practice in medieval Orthodoxy. At that time, however, it had not been definitively formulated, though the fathers of the Council of a Hundred Chapters, in the mid-sixteenth century, were already close to doing so. It is no accident that Florensky uses the materials of this council as a guide in his *Iconostasis*.

The iconographic canon of medieval Orthodox art embraced virtually the entire system of artistic means of expression. Compositional schemes; the organization of space; figures, attitudes, gestures; the forms of nearly all objects, as well as their choice; color, light, the manner of painting *lichnóe* and *dolíchnoe* [these terms will be explained below], and so on—everything in the icon was canonized, and each canonized element and technique had its profound significance. Fr. Paul's sharp mind did not overlook any of them.

The scope and purpose of the present essay prevent us from going into this subject in detail. It calls for a separate study. Yet it would be wrong to omit it entirely, as that would significantly narrow our conception of Florensky's aesthetic views. He approaches each apparently quite inconspicuous element and technique of iconography as a thinker—that is, perceiving the deep meaning, the special significance of each of them. He regarded none of these things as accidental; behind each he saw the long process of historical creativity leading to its existence in canonized form. It was Florensky's firm conviction that behind the profoundly and substantially developed system of iconographic portrayal there stood "the basic principles of a universally human metaphysics and gnoseology, the natural way of seeing and understanding the world." This he opposed to the western (Renaissance) artistic vision which, together with its techniques of expression, he considered artificial.

Florensky perceived in the icon an integral image of being, and saw the process of its creation as a repetition of the major "steps of divine creation." This is why he called iconography "visual ontology."

In the language of the iconographers, the icon as a whole consists of two types of painting, *lichnóe* and *dolíchnoe*—literally, "facial" and "pre-facial." The first refers to the depiction of the face and the uncovered parts of the body (hands and feet), the second to all the rest— clothing, landscape, architecture, and so on. Florensky finds it remarkable that the old iconographers included with the face "those secondary members of expression, those smaller faces of our being—the hands and feet." In the division of the pictorial structure of the icon into *lichnóe* and *dolíchnoe*, he sees the long patristic and ancient Greek tradition of understanding being as a harmony of man and nature, of internal and external. In the icon, they are inseparable, yet they cannot be considered the same. It was precisely this harmony, Florensky believes, which was violated in the new European painting with its separation of portrait and landscape into independent genres. In the first, man was removed from nature; in the second, the natural surroundings of man were absolutized. "The icon, on the contrary, preserves the balance of the two principles, but gives first place to the king and bridegroom of nature—the person—while the whole of nature, the kingdom and the bride, takes second place."

The painting of an icon, Florensky emphasizes, begins, as did the creation of the world, with *light*—the golden background from which, "as from a sea of golden blessedness," the images of the icon itself emerge, "washed by streams of divine light." The whole surface of the icon is covered with gold, except for those parts on which the outline of the future images has been incised. A golden light surrounds the white silhouettes of those images, which are nothing as yet, but are already intended to receive artistic being. There follows the process of painting the *dolíchnoe* (like the creation of the whole natural world), which is done in consecutive stages, in a way fundamentally different, as Florensky thought, from painting in oils. The white silhouettes are first filled in with a dark wash of some basic color, covering all the *dolíchnoe*. Brushstrokes and glazing are impossible in iconography, both technically and in terms of world view—here "reality emerges through stages of the revealing of being, it is not an accretion of separate parts, it is not formed by putting pieces or qualities together." Then comes the painting proper, of the drapery and other elements, in the same color but of a bright shade, more permeated with light. There follow several stages or layers of the consecutive lightening of the *dolíchnoe*—that is, the superimposing of gradually lightening tones of color—and finally the addition of white touches, or "enliveners," on highlighted areas. The painting of the *dolíchnoe* is completed by the applying of gold lines to certain parts of the garments (not always and not on all figures). The creation of an icon begins with light and ends with light: "The icon begins with the gold of creative blessedness and ends with the gold of sanctifying blessedness."

The *lichnóe* in an icon is painted last, as opposed to oil painting, which begins with the face. The process here is essentially the same as for the *dolíchnoe*—from dark basic tones, through consecutive layers of lighter color, to a re-drawing of facial details and the addition of "enliveners," bright touches on highlighted or "structurally" important parts of the face. In his work, the iconographer proceeds "from the dark to the light, from darkness to light"; he creates an image as if from nothing, thus resembling the divine Creator.

Everything in an icon has its meaning, specifically its artistic meaning, even such apparently insignificant elements as the size of the board or the composition of the varnish with which the completed work is covered. The size of the board fundamentally influences the whole artistic harmony of the icon, while the varnish not only serves to preserve the paint but brings the colors "to a unity of general tone," lending them a special depth, a golden warmth. An icon that is coated with a new, colorless varnish after restoration loses something significant in its artistic appearance; it acquires the look "of some sort of priming for a future work."

As has already been mentioned, Florensky devoted a long separate work to "inverse perspective," the whole system of special methods by which the imagery in an icon is organized. After analyzing many examples of "deviation" from the rules of direct perspective, examples of "incorrectness" and "naivety" from the point of view of the new European school of art, Fr. Pavel came to the conclusion that they are in no case accidental and proceed not from a want of skill in the old masters but from the artistic laws of a special system of depiction. In such "incorrectnesses" as the radiating of parallel lines from the lower to the upper edge of the icon (and not vice versa, as in "renaissance" painting), the enlargement of figures in the background, the multiplicity of points of view on the object (as if it were unfolding towards the viewer), the difference in color of the front and side walls of buildings, the use of "unnatural" colors, and so on, Florensky sees not the weakness but the strength of iconography, its "amazing expressiveness" and fullness, its "aesthetic fruitfulness." This system of methods, subtly developed over the centuries, is determined by the metaphysics of the icon, by the tasks it was called upon to fulfill within the system of Orthodox culture, of which we have already spoken above.

In particular, Florensky gives much attention to gold in his reflections, to the applying of gold lines to the iconographic image. Gold, being a metal, "a substance completely foreign to paint," is very difficult to bring into harmony with the color system of an icon, and yet it is firmly established in iconographic practice. If colors express themselves as reflecting light, gold is itself "pure, unalloyed light." Visually, paint and gold "are defined as belonging to different spheres of being," and iconography makes use precisely of this difference.

The lines of gold applied to a garment or a seat do not

correspond to any visible lines of the object (folds in the material, the outlines of planes, and so on). Florensky is convinced that they represent the system of potential lines of the inner energetic structure of the object, similar to the lines of force of an electric or magnetic field. "They express the metaphysical scheme of a given object, its dynamics, with greater force than do its visible lines, but in themselves they are invisible, and, being painted on an icon, constitute in the iconographer's design a totality of instructions for the contemplating eye—the lines of movement the eye is instructed to follow as it contemplates the icon."

This gold is by no means applied to all the objects depicted in an icon. Their number is limited, for the most part, to the Savior's garments (whether as an infant or as an adult), the Holy Gospel, the throne of the Savior, the seats of the angels in the depiction of the Trinity, and the footstool of Christ and the angels in the same icon. Thus, as Fr. Pavel emphasizes, the lines of gold are applied only to that "which is directly related to divine power," "to direct manifestations of the divine energy," "to direct revelations of divine grace." Generally speaking, gold in an icon symbolizes the divine light. In a similar way, Florensky analyzes many other elements of the icon.

In conclusion I would like to emphasize that in the person of the greatest religious thinker and seer of the first half of this century, Orthodox aesthetic consciousness, which had almost died out by the end of the seventeenth century and showed only faint glimmers over the next two centuries in the hidden depths of certain Russian monasteries and in the souls of certain isolated seekers of patristic Truth, suddenly acquired a strong and fervently youthful voice. At the dawn of a new cultural era, Pavel Florensky gave clear and distinct formulation to all that this consciousness had lived by throughout the medieval period, and presented the spiritual revelations of Orthodoxy, enriched by the most recent intellectual experience, to mankind of the nascent scientific-technological age in an accessible and comprehensible language.

Appendix

Pavel Florensky on the "Trinity"
of Andrey Rublev

...But if the church was dedicated to the Most Holy Trinity, then an icon of the Holy Trinity also had to stand in it, expressing the spiritual essence of the church—its name, so to speak, realized in colors. Here it is hard to imagine that the disciple of St Sergius's disciple, his spiritual grandson as it were, almost his contemporary, who had been working in his lifetime and probably knew him personally, would dare to supplant the composition of the icon of the Trinity that existed in the Saint's time and was established by him, with the disciple's own arbitrary composition of the same proto-type. Miniatures of the life of Epiphanius show icons of the Trinity in St Sergius's cell not at the very beginning but only from the middle of his life; that is, they testify to its appearance precisely in the midst of the Saint's activity. If the prototypal icon of Sophia, unknown to Byzantium, was first created in Kievan Rus, at its very beginning, going back to the vision of the child Cyril, the knight of Sophia, then the icon of the Trinity, pre-viously unknown to the world, first appeared in the Muscovite period of Russia, again at its very beginning, and artistically embodied the spiritual contemplation of the servant of the Most Holy Trinity—Sergius. We have said, "unknown to the world," yet here, too, as in our statements about the Trinitarian council, we must distinguish between spiritual meaning as symbolic content and those historically produced materials that pertain to the embodying of the symbol. If we speak of the latter with regard to Rublev's famous Trinity, then of course it must be considered merely as a link in the chain of development of pictorial art in general and of the composition of the three Angel-Sojourners in particular. The history of this composition is very long, for already in the year 314, as Julian Africanus reports, there was near the oak of Mamre a picture portraying the appearance of the three sojourners to Abraham, and similar depictions are known from the fifth and sixth centuries on the walls of Santa Maria Maggiore in Rome and the church of St Vitalius in Ravenna. Since then this iconographic subject has occurred repeatedly; but one must grasp the spiritual meaning of these depictions before establishing their connection with Rublev's Trinity. The portrayal of a woman with a child in her arms is not at all a prototype of the Sistine Madonna, for what created her was by no means the theme of motherhood, which is available to anyone, but precisely the God-motherhood revealed to Raphael. In the same way, three figures around a dinner table, even if they are furnished with wings, simply cannot be compared with the Trinity of Rublev, for what is creative in this icon is not in the least defined by this subject. The compositions of the three Sojourners with Abraham standing before them, or later without him, is no more than an episode from Abraham's life, even though it later became generally accepted to see it as an allusion to the Most Holy Trinity. In Rublev's work, we are moved, struck, and almost burned, not by the subject, not by the number "three," not by the cup on the table, nor by the wings, but by the sudden tearing away of the curtain of the noumenal world before our eyes. On the aesthetic level what is important for us is not how the iconographer achieved this baring of the noumenal, or whether the same paints or the same methods were in someone else's hands, but that he truly conveyed to us the revelation he beheld. Amid the restless conditions of his time, amid strife and internal dissension, universal savagery and Tartar raids, amid this deep peacelessness that ravaged Russia, an infinite, imperturbable, inviolable peace, a "peace from above," from the world on high, was revealed to his spiritual sight. To the enmity and hatred reigning below there is opposed this mutual love, flowing in eternal harmony, in eternal silent conversation, in the eternal unity of the lofty spheres. It is this inexplicable peace pouring from Rublev's Trinity in a broad stream directly into the soul of the contemplator, this azure to which nothing in the world can compare—more sky-blue than our own sky itself; yes, this truly trans-heavenly azure, the ineffable dream of Lermontov, who yearned for it—this inexpressible graciousness of the mutually inclined figures, this trans-worldly silence of wordlessness, this boundless obedience before each other, that we consider to be the creative content of the Trinity. Human culture, represented by the building; the world of life, represented by the tree; the earth, represented by the cliff—all is small and insignificant before this communion of inexhaustible, infinite love; it all merely exists around it and for its sake—for by its blueness, by the music of its beauty, by its being above sex, above age, above all earthly definitions and distinctions, it is heaven itself, is unconditional reality itself, is that truly best which is higher than all that exists. Andrey Rublev made incarnate a vision of the world which is as inconceivable as it is crystallinely firm and unshakeably true. But in order to see this world, in order to take into his soul and brush this cool, life-giving breath of the spirit, the artist had to have the heavenly prototype before him, and around him its earthly reflection; he had to be in a spiritual, in a peaceful environment. As an artist Andrey Rublev was nourished by what had been given him. And therefore it is not St Andrey Rublev, the spiritual grandson of St Sergius, but the father of the Russian land—Sergius of Radonezh himself—who must be revered as the true creator of the greatest work, not only of Russian, but quite certainly of all world art. In the icon of the Trinity, Andrey Rublev was not an independent creator, but only the inspired executor of the creative design and fundamental composition given him by St Sergius. This is the second symbol of the Russian spirit; later Russian history unfolds under its sign, and it is worth noting—though we could expect nothing else—that the great liturgical progress through which in due course the Russian idea and the peculiar features of the Russian spirit were expressed, is again connected with the name of St Sergius...

From "The Trinity-St Sergius Monastery and Russia,"
					1919

Bibliographical Note

Victor Vasilievich Bychkov's essay *Esteticheskiy lik bytiya* (*Umozreniya Pavla Florenskogo*), published by Znanie (Moscow, 1990) as one of a series of popular scholarly brochures, has only a limited number of footnotes and is without critical apparatus.

Apart from a few fragments, the works of Pavel Florensky have not been translated into English. Those interested in tracing Prof. Bychkov's numerous citations to their original sources will find most of them in Florensky's writings on art or in his major early work, *The Pillar and Foundation of the Truth,* published as volumes I and IV of the YMCA Press edition of Florensky's works (Paris, 1985 and 1989) under the general editorship of N. A. Struve. Florensky's lecture on "Mysteries and Rites," cited by Prof. Bychkov in his chapter on "Cult," was published in an English translation by Larissa Volokhonsky and Richard Pevear in *St. Vladimir's Theological Quarterly,* vol. 30, No. 4 (1986). A short version of Florensky's *Ikonostas,* entitled "The Icon," was published in an English translation by John L. Opie in *Eastern Churches Review*, VIII (1976).